Workbook and Anthology

for use with

Harmony in Context

Miguel A. Roig-Francolí
University of Cincinnati

Boston   Burr Ridge, IL   Dubuque, IA   Madison, WI   New York   San Francisco   St. Louis
Bangkok   Bogotá   Caracas   Kuala Lumpur   Lisbon   London   Madrid   Mexico City
Milan   Montreal   New Delhi   Santiago   Seoul   Singapore   Sydney   Taipei   Toronto

McGraw-Hill Higher Education

*A Division of The **McGraw-Hill** Companies*

Workbook and Anthology for use with
HARMONY IN CONTEXT
Miguel A. Roig-Francolí

6 7 8 9 0 QPD/QPD 0 9 8 7 6 5

ISBN 0-07-303998-5

www.mhhe.com

Preface

This workbook is meant to be used in conjunction with the study of the textbook *Harmony in Context*. The textbook provides, at the end of each chapter, a set of exercises in the form of a worksheet. A second set of exercises for each chapter is provided in this workbook. Exercises here are similar to, but not always of the exact same type as, those found in the corresponding worksheet. Both sets for each chapter begin with several analytical exercises, followed by writing and composition exercises of many types: chord spelling and recognition, realization of short and long progressions based on given Roman numerals, realization of figured basses, harmonization of melodies, composition of keyboard-style accompaniments, composition of original harmonic progressions, and so on. Instructors may wish to use one of the two sets for practice in class, and the other one for homework assignments, or they may choose to use one of the sets as a pool of possible questions to be used in quizzes and exams.

Chapters also include an assignment of keyboard harmony in which the chords and most standard progressions studied in each chapter are practiced at the piano in a variety of keys. Playing and practicing these keyboard exercises will reinforce the understanding of the harmonic materials studied in the book, and will help students familiarize themselves with the sound of specific harmonic progressions.

Finally, this volume also includes an anthology of more than sixty musical excerpts and complete pieces by twenty-seven different composers ranging from the sixteenth century to the twentieth century. The anthology is widely used as a source of examples from the literature throughout both the textbook and the workbook, and it allows for analyses of and references to numerous complete pieces or movements which otherwise could not have been addressed. Because of this close relationship between the book and the anthology, the latter is not meant to be an optional supplement to the book, but rather an essential and required component of the pedagogical packet.

Contents

Harmony
harmony in Context
Workbook

INTRODUCTION

The Fundamentals
of Music

Chapter A

Pitch: Notation and Intervals

EXERCISE A.1   Notate the following notes on the grand staff, in the correct octave.

E2   B♭5   G♯4   A1   C3   E♭4   A♭5   F6   D7   B4   C♯6   E5   F♯2   G3   D♭5   C2

EXERCISE A.2

1. In exercise A.2a write P4s *above and below* each of the given notes.
2. In exercise A.2b write P5s *above and below* each of the given notes.
3. In exercise A.2c write M3s *above and below* each of the given notes.
4. In exercise A.2d write m3s *above and below* each of the given notes.

a. P4   b. P5

c. M3   d. m3

EXERCISE A.10   Refer back to exercise A.6. Under each of the intervals in this exercise, write a C or a D depending on whether the interval is consonant (C) or dissonant (D).

EXERCISE A.11   In the following melodic examples from the literature, identify each of the numbered intervals by size and quality.

♪ Example A.1a   Johann Sebastian Bach, Fugue 20 in Am, from *The Well-Tempered Clavier*, II, mm. 6–9

♪ Example A.1b   J. S. Bach, "Kyrie," from Mass in Bm, mm. 5–7

♪ Example A.1c   Béla Bartok, "Chromatic Invention," from *Mikrokosmos*, no. 91, mm 3–6

EXERCISE A.12   Identify the numbered intervals in the following example. What characteristic can you recognize in this succession of intervals? (How many different intervals are there in this phrase?) How are intervals 1–6 related to intervals 6–11?

Example A.2   Alban Berg, *Lyric Suite,* I, mm. 2–4

Chapter B

Rhythm and Meter

EXERCISE B.1 Supply the information required in the blanks.

_____ ♪ notes = 2 𝅝 notes | A 𝄾 rest = _____ 𝄿 rests

_____ 𝅗𝅥 notes = 6 ♩ notes | A ▬ rest = _____ 𝄾 rests

_____ 𝅘𝅥𝅯 notes = 1 𝅗𝅥 note | A ▪ rest = _____ ▬ rests

_____ 𝅘𝅥𝅰 notes = 3 𝅘𝅥𝅯 notes | A 𝄿 rest = _____ 𝄾 rests

EXERCISE B.2 For each of the following patterns, write the equivalent duration with only one note value. (You will need dots in some cases.)

♩ ♩ ♩ =   𝅘𝅥𝅯𝅘𝅥𝅯𝅘𝅥𝅯𝅘𝅥𝅯𝅘𝅥𝅯𝅘𝅥𝅯 =

♫ =   𝅘𝅥𝅰𝅘𝅥𝅰𝅘𝅥𝅰 =

𝅘𝅥𝅯𝅘𝅥𝅯𝅘𝅥𝅯𝅘𝅥𝅯𝅘𝅥𝅯𝅘𝅥𝅯 =   ♩   ♪ =

♩ ♫ =   ♩. ♩ =

7

EXERCISE B.3   Show, by means of tied notes (as few as possible in each case), the value of each dotted or doubly dotted note.

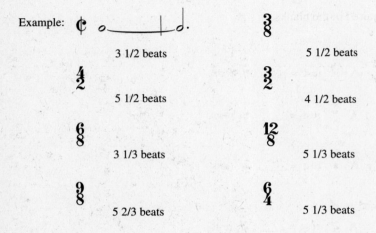

EXERCISE B.4   Using the fewest possible notes, along with ties where needed, write a single duration lasting the number of beats specified in each of the following cases. Include bar lines if more than one measure is needed.

Example:

¢   3 1/2 beats

3/8   5 1/2 beats

4/2   5 1/2 beats

3/2   4 1/2 beats

6/8   3 1/3 beats

12/8   5 1/3 beats

9/8   5 2/3 beats

6/4   5 1/3 beats

EXERCISE B.5   Write an appropriate meter signature for each of the following examples.

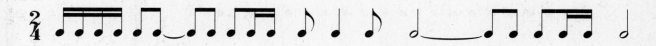

EXERCISE B.6   Add bar lines to the following examples.

EXERCISE B.7   Correct the notation of the following examples so that the beaming clarifies the meter and rhythm.

a.

b.

EXERCISE B.8   Add ties to the following examples, in order to

1. Create syncopations in a.
2. Create hemiolas in b.

a.

b.

EXERCISE B.9   Transcribe the following melody from $\frac{3}{4}$ to $\frac{3}{8}$ and $\frac{3}{2}$.

Anna Amalie

Chapter C

Tonality: Scales, Keys, and Transposition

EXERCISE C.1   Identify the following *major and minor* key signatures.

EXERCISE C.2   Write the following *major and minor* key signatures. Make sure to write sharps and flats in the correct order, and to place them in the correct location on the staff.

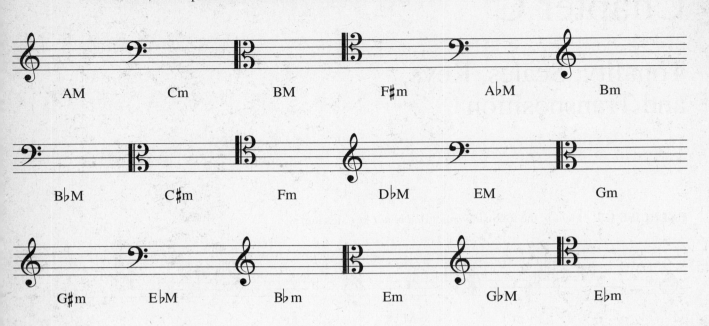

AM   Cm   BM   F#m   AbM   Bm

BbM   C#m   Fm   DbM   EM   Gm

G#m   EbM   Bbm   Em   GbM   Ebm

EXERCISE C.3   Write the following *major and minor* scales without using key signatures (use accidentals before each note as needed). The tonic for each scale is given.

Natural minor   Harmonic minor

Major   Melodic minor (ascending and descending)

Harmonic minor   Melodic minor (ascending and descending)

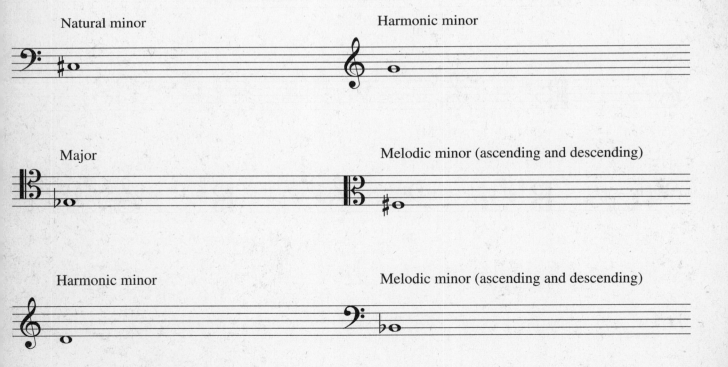

EXERCISE C.4 Identify the following *modal* signatures, given the signature and the tonic. In all cases, these are transposed Church mode signatures.

EXERCISE C.5 Write the following transposed modal scales without using signatures (write accidentals before each note as needed).

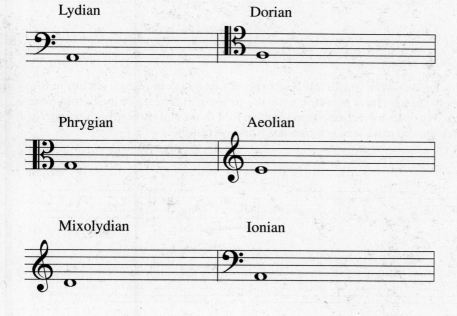

EXERCISE C.6 Transpose the following melody to the required intervals. In each case, first determine what the transposed key will be. Then, write the transposed key signature and, finally, transpose the pitches to the required interval. Can you use any of the clefs you have learned so far to help you realize any of these transpositions?

1. Up a M2 in exercise C.6.a.

2. Down a P4 in exercise C.6.b.

3. Up a m3 in exercise C.6.c.

EXERCISE C.7

1. Suppose that you need to write the following British folk tune to be performed in unison by a clarinet in B♭, a horn in F, and an alto saxophone. In the spaces provided, write the correct part for each of these instruments as they would have to perform it in order for the melody to sound in E♭M as notated in the given version. Notice any accidentals in this melody, and make sure you transpose them correctly.

2. Suppose that the following Spanish folk melody is to be performed as notated by a clarinet in A, a trumpet in D, and a soprano saxophone. Write, in the spaces provided, what the melody would sound like as played by each of these instruments.

EXERCISE C.8 Sing or play each of the following melodies. Then, analyze the melody to determine the following items: tonic pitch, tonic triad, range, tonal frame, mode or key, and scale.

Write in each of the items in the spaces provided under each melody. This same process is illustrated in example C.1 of the textbook, and in exercise C.9a in worksheet C.

For the item "mode or key," the following options are possible: Any major or minor key, any of the Church modes (Dorian, Phrygian, etc.), pentatonic, or whole tone. Among the scales, the chromatic scale is also a possibility (in the context of any major or minor key).

a.

Denmark

TONIC   TONIC TRIAD   RANGE   TONAL FRAME   MODE / KEY   SCALE:

Pan - ge   lin - gua   glo - ri - o - si

Plainchant

TONIC   TONIC TRIAD   RANGE   TONAL FRAME   MODE / KEY   SCALE:

Chapter E

The Rudiments of Harmony I:
Triads and Seventh Chords

EXERCISE E.1 Identify and label the following triads by root and type (M, m, °, +), and label each triad as shown in the example.

EXERCISE E.2 Write the indicated triads in root position. A triad member (root, third, or fifth) is given. Identify the root for each triad, and notate it under the triad type, as indicated in the given examples.

Third Given

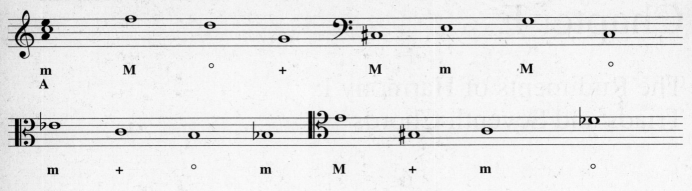

Fifth Given

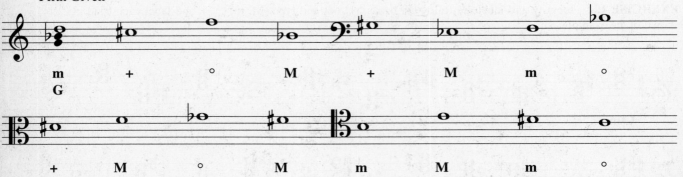

EXERCISE E.3   In a major key, the diatonic triad on scale degree

$\hat{2}$ is: M / m / ° / $^+$ *(circle one)*

$\hat{7}$ is: M / m / ° / $^+$

$\hat{3}$ is: M / m / ° / $^+$

$\hat{1}$ is: M / m / ° / $^+$

$\hat{6}$ is: M / m / ° / $^+$

$\hat{5}$ is: M / m / ° / $^+$

$\hat{4}$ is: M / m / ° / $^+$

In a minor key, the following are the most usual diatonic triads, which result from the harmonic-minor scale (with the only exception of the chord on $\hat{3}$, which includes a ♭$\hat{7}$):

The triad on $\hat{2}$ is: M / m / ° / $^+$

$\hat{7}$ is: M / m / ° / $^+$

$\hat{3}$ is: M / m / ° / $^+$

$\hat{1}$ is: M / m / ° / $^+$

$\hat{6}$ is: M / m / ° / $^+$

$\hat{5}$ is: M / m / ° / $^+$

$\hat{4}$ is: M / m / ° / $^+$

EXERCISE E.4   Write the following M, m, or ° triads in *first inversion* on the given bass (the third of the chord). Identify the root for each triad, and notate it under the triad type, as indicated in the given example.

EXERCISE E.5   Write the following M or m triads in *second inversion* on the given bass (the fifth of the chord). Identify the root for each triad, and notate it under the triad type, as indicated in the given example.

EXERCISE E.6   The following triads are in first or second inversion. Identify the root, the type, and the inversion for each of them, and label each triad as shown in the example. Your labels should be of the following type: Dm₆, GM⁶₄, E°₆, F⁺⁶₄, etc.

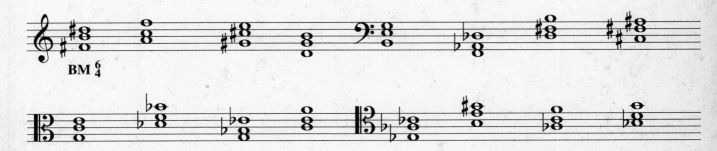

EXERCISE E.7   Identify and label the following seventh chords by type (Mm, MM, mm, $\varnothing$, $\circ$).

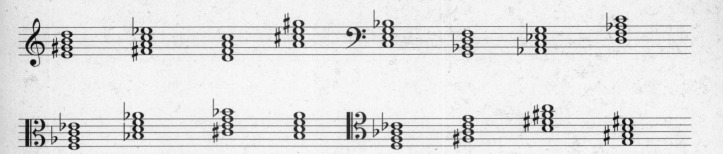

EXERCISE E.8   Write the indicated seventh chords in root position. The root is given.

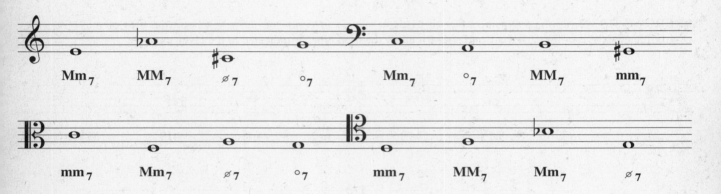

EXERCISE E.9   Identify the following chord types and inversions. Notice that both triads and seventh chords are included in this exercise. Label each chord with the usual chord-type symbols and with figures to indicate inversion, and also write down its root (e.g., M_4^6/A, Mm_3^4/G, mm_5^6/D, m_6/F, etc.).

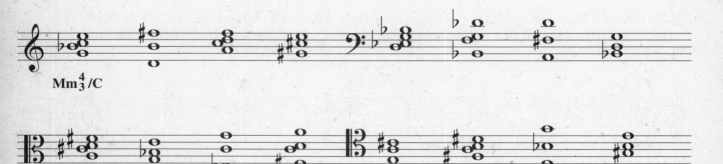

EXERCISE E.10   Refer to the passage by J. S. Bach reproduced in example E.1. Fourteen chords are numbered. Study each of the chords, and determine whether it is consonant or dissonant, a triad or a seventh chord, the root and type of chord (DM, Cm, EMm$_7$, Fmm$_7$, etc.), and the appropriate figures to indicate the chord's position ($\frac{5}{3}$, $\frac{6}{3}$, $\frac{6}{4}$, 7, $\frac{6}{5}$, $\frac{4}{3}$, etc.). You may provide all of the above information in the following chart (the information for chord 1 has been provided as an example).

♪ Example E.1   J. S. Bach, Chorale 334, "Für deinen Thron tret' ich hiermit," mm. 1–8

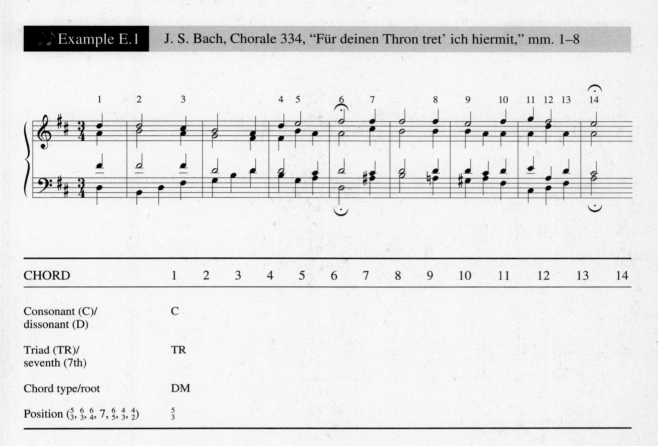

CHORD	1	2	3	4	5	6	7	8	9	10	11	12	13	14
Consonant (C)/ dissonant (D)	C													
Triad (TR)/ seventh (7th)	TR													
Chord type/root	DM													
Position ($\frac{5}{3}$, $\frac{6}{3}$, $\frac{6}{4}$, 7, $\frac{6}{5}$, $\frac{4}{3}$, 2)	$\frac{5}{3}$													

KEYBOARD EXERCISES   Play the following exercises at the keyboard with the right hand. Examples for each of the exercises are provided in example E.2.

1. Be able to play M, m, ° and $^{+}$ triads in root position on any note.

2. Be able to play the diatonic triads on each of the scale degrees in the following keys:

    CM, GM, FM, DM, and B♭M

    Am, Em, Dm, Bm, and Gm

    In minor keys, use the harmonic minor scale (except for the triad on $\hat{3}$, which you should play as a M triad)

3. Play the following triads in first inversion:

CM, GM, FM, DM, B♭M, AM, E♭M, EM, A♭M, BM D♭M, F♯M

Am, Em, Dm, Bm, Gm, F♯m, Cm, C♯m, Fm, G♯m, B♭m, D♯m

4. Play the same triads in second inversion.

Example E.2

1.

2.

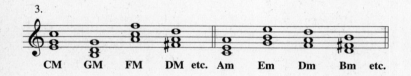

3.

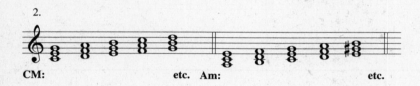

4.

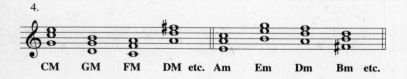

Chapter F

The Rudiments of Harmony II: Labeling Chords

EXERCISE F.1   Write the triads represented by the following Roman numerals in the given keys.

DM: V   ii   I   vi   FM: IV   vii°   iii   V   E♭M: ii   vi   I   IV

Gm: iv   vii°   V   III   Em: ii°   VI   iv   V   Am: III   vii°   V   ii°

BM: vi   IV   ii   V   A♭M: I   iii   V   vii°

EXERCISE F.2   Write the following diatonic triads above the given bass notes. Triads are here represented by a Roman numeral (and a figure to indicate an inversion) in a given key. Identify the root for each triad, and notate it under the triad type, as indicated in the given example.

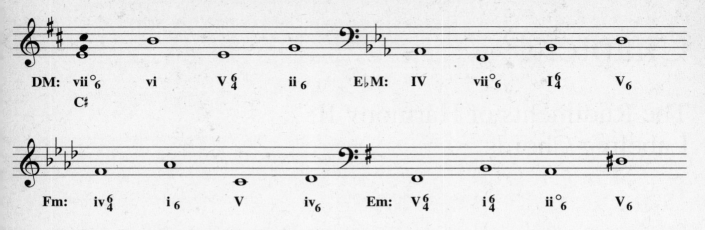

DM: vii°₆   vi   V ⁶₄   ii ₆   E♭M: IV   vii°₆   I ⁶₄   V₆
C♯

Fm: iv ⁶₄   i ₆   V   iv₆   Em: V ⁶₄   i ⁶₄   ii°₆   V₆

EXERCISE F.3   Write the following diatonic triads, indicated by Roman numerals, in the given key.

Gm: i ₆   V ⁶₄   iv   vii°₆   Bm: ii°₆   iv ⁶₄   V₆   III

AM: I ⁶₄   vii°₆   IV₆   ii   B♭M: V₆   ii₆   vi   IV ⁶₄

EXERCISE F.4   Provide the Roman numeral and position for the following triads in the given keys. Triads may appear in root position or inversion. Your labels should be of the following types, as shown in the example: V ⁶₄, ii₆, IV, vii°₆, etc.

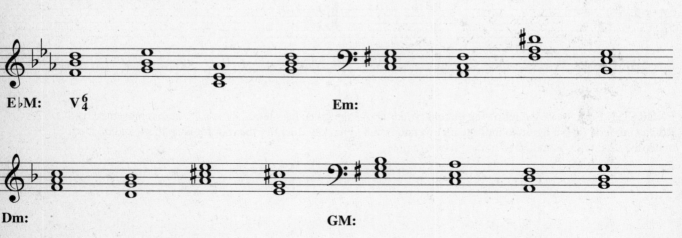

E♭M: V ⁶₄   Em:

Dm: GM:

EXERCISE F.5   Write the seventh chords represented by the following Roman numerals in the given keys.

EXERCISE F.6   Realize the following isolated figured bass chords. Items a and b are all triads, and you will need only two upper voices to notate a complete chord. Items c and d are all seventh chords, and you will need three upper voices for complete sonorities.

EXERCISE F.7   Analyze the following chorale by J. S. Bach with figured bass symbols. That is, imagine that you want to write a figured bass reduction of this chorale for a keyboard player, using exactly Bach's harmonies. Under the chorale, notate the exact figures you would need to have in your figured bass.

Example F.1   J. S. Bach, Chorale 204, "Wer weiβ, wie nahe mir," mm. 1–5

EXERCISE F.8   Refer to the passage by Mozart reproduced in example F.2. Seven chords are boxed and numbered. Study each chord, and determine whether it is consonant or dissonant, a triad or a seventh chord, its position, and, for all chords except chord 3, the complete Roman numeral (with figures indicating position, e.g., ii_6) in the key of CM. Provide all of the above information in the following chart (the information for chord 1 has been provided as an example).

Example F.2   Wolfgang Amadeus Mozart, Piano Sonata in CM, K. 309, III, mm. 9–17

CHORD	1	2	3	4	5	6	7
Consonant (C)/ dissonant (D)	C						
Triad (TR)/ seventh (7th)	TR						
Position ($\frac{5}{3}$, $\frac{6}{3}$, $\frac{6}{4}$, 7, $\frac{6}{5}$, $\frac{4}{3}$, $\frac{4}{2}$)	$\frac{5}{3}$						
Chord	1	2	3	4	5	6	7
Roman numerals in CM	I	X					

KEYBOARD EXERCISES   Play the following exercises at the keyboard with the right hand. Examples for each of the exercises are provided in example F.3.

1. Play the triads represented by the following Roman numerals in each of the following M keys:

   I, V, ii, vii°, IV, vi, iii

   CM, GM, FM, DM, AND B♭M

   Play the triads represented by the following Roman numerals in each of the following m keys:

   i, iv, VI, V, vii°, III, ii°

   Am, Em, Dm, Bm, and Gm

2. Play the following chords in each of the keys from exercise 1:

   M: I_6, V_6, ii_6, $vii°_6$ IV_6, vi_6, iii_6

   m: i_6, iv_6, VI_6, $vii°_6$ III_6, $ii°_6$

3. Play the following chords in each of the keys from keyboard exercise 1:

   M: I_4^6, IV_4^6, V_4^6

   m: i_4^6, iv_4^6, V_4^6

Example F.3

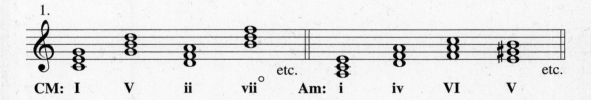

1.

CM: I   V   ii   vii°   etc.   Am: i   iv   VI   V   etc.

♪ Example F.3   Continued

2.

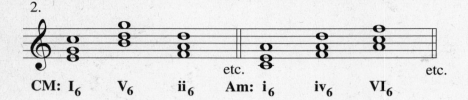

CM: I₆   V₆   ii₆   Am: i₆   iv₆   VI₆

3.

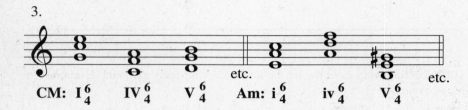

CM: I⁶₄   IV⁶₄   V⁶₄   Am: i⁶₄   iv⁶₄   V⁶₄

PART 1

Diatonic Harmony

Chapter 1

The Connection of Chords

EXERCISE 1.1 Study the part writing and voice leading in the following examples from Bach chorales. Identify one case of each of the listed events, and label each one with the corresponding "event number" (1, 2, 3, etc.) with an arrow pointing at the exact location of the event. For each example of chord connection, write "yes" or "no" to indicate whether Bach follows our guidelines for voice leading according to the corresponding root motion.

1. Example 1.1.
    1. A root-position chord connection with root motion by descending 5th (or ascending 4th).
    2. A root-position chord connection with root motion by step.
    3. A root-position chord connection with root motion by 3rd.
    4. A root-position chord connection with root motion by ascending 5th (or descending 4th).
    5. A chord in open position.
    6. A chord in close position.
    7. A V–I progression in GM in which the LT resolves to Î in the same voice.

| ♪ Example 1.1 | J. S. Bach, Chorale 102, "Ermuntre dich, mein schwacher Geist," mm. 1–8 |

EXERCISE 1.4   Complete the following progressions in four voices. All your chords should be in root position, and you should apply the principles of voice leading according to root motion which we studied in this chapter.

EXERCISE 1.5   Write a melody in good style, following the guidelines for melodic style discussed in this chapter.

Chapter 2

The Tonic and Dominant Triads in Root Position

EXERCISE 2.1   *Analysis.* Study example 2.1.

1. What is the key of the piece (Careful: note that this little dance piece does not begin on the tonic)?

2. Analyze the complete example with Roman numerals (RN). Notice that the left hand uses the *bass after-beat* keyboard pattern, and that *the complete measure* is analyzed as one chord, with the position determined by the bass on the downbeat.

    a) On what harmony does this piece begin?

    b) On what two chords is the piece based?

    c) The first section of the piece (mm. 1–8) has two phrases (1–4 and 5–8). Is there any difference between the two phrases? What kind of cadence occurs in mm. 4 and 8?

    d) The second section (mm. 9–16) also contains two phrases (9–12 and 13–16). How are they related? Are the cadences in mm. 12 and 16 the same? Identify the cadence type for both of them.

    e) Is the complete melody based on a short rhythmic pattern (a rhythmic motive)? Write this rhythmic pattern here:

KEYBOARD PROGRESSIONS   Play the following keyboard progressions and listen to the chords and their connections as you play. Play them in several keys. Begin with CM and Cm, and then play them in major and minor modes on G, D, and F (except for example 2.2a, which you should be able to play in all M and m keys).

Example 2.2

Notice that these progressions are written in *keyboard texture,* rather than four-part vocal texture. In chordal keyboard texture, it is customary to play the bass alone with the left hand, and the three remaining voices in close position with the right hand. All the same voice-leading rules studied in this and the previous chapters apply to keyboard block-chord style.

Chapter 3

Harmonic Function; The Subdominant Triad in Root Position

EXERCISE 3.1   Analysis.

1. Example 3.1.

   a) Analyze the passage with RNs (Roman numerals).

   b) What is the function of the chord in m. 100? Explain its voice leading, and how it relates to the previous and following chord.

   c) Study the voice leading for the whole passage, focusing especially on the right hand. Does it conform with the voice-leading guidelines we studied in chapters 2 and 3?

2. Example 3.2. Study the progression in this excerpt. Analyze it with RNs. Compare its voice leading with the voice leading for this progression studied in this chapter, and comment on your comparison.

3. Anthology, no. 56 (Clara Schumann, Trio). On what type of cadence does Clara Schumann end this piece? Can you identify any specific voice-leading licenses taken in the left hand of the piano (mm. 284–285)? This type of open voicing is characteristic for the lower register of the piano, and open fifths provide a very strong harmonic support for such broad instrumental sonorities. The deliberate parallel voicing used here by C. Schumann may be found in instrumental writing, and should not be considered a voice-leading "mistake."

EXERCISE 3.4   Each of the following melodies is made up of two melodic patterns which in this chapter have been associated with specific harmonic patterns. Harmonize each of the melodies with one of the following progressions: I–IV–V–I–IV–I; I–V–I–IV–I–V; or I–IV–I–IV–V–I, matching the progressions with the respective melodic patterns. Besides looking for patterns, also make sure that the progression you choose is the correct one to harmonize each particular melody by checking each pitch from the melody with the corresponding RN. Write only bass line and RNs under each melody (you need not add inner voices). Begin by singing each melody, and play each two-voice harmonization after you write it.

FM: DM:

KEYBOARD PROGRESSIONS   Play the following keyboard progressions in the following major keys: C, F, G, and D; and in the following minor keys: C, A, D, and E.

♪ Example 3.3

Chapter 4

Texture; Triads in First Inversion

EXERCISE 4.1   Analysis.

1. *Texture.* On a separate sheet, briefly discuss the texture of the following examples:
   a) Anthology, no. 32, Beethoven, Piano Sonata in Fm, op. 2, no. 1, mm. 1–8.
   b) Anthology, no. 22, Chevalier de Saint–Georges, Violin Concerto.
   c) Anthology, no. 27, Mozart, Piano Sonata in AM, mm. 1–8.
   d) Anthology, no. 26, Mozart, Piano Sonata in CM, III.
   e) Example 4.1.
   f) Example 4.2.

In each of these examples, ask yourself and answer the following questions:

1) Is it homophonic or polyphonic (contrapuntal)?
2) If it is homophonic, what kind of accompaniment does it feature?
   a. Melody with block chords.
   b. Melody with broken (arpeggiated) chords.

♪♪ Example 4.1   Antonio de Cabezón, Psalm Tone Verset, Mode 1

Example 4.2   A. de Cabezón, *Diferencias sobre el Canto del Caballero*

    c. Melody, chords, and a parallel supporting melody.

    d. Accompaniment (mostly) homorhythmic with melody.

    e. Other (explain).

3) Is an outer-voice contrapuntal frame evident in each of these homophonic examples?

4) If it is polyphonic, explain the exact relationship among voices.

    a. Chorale texture.

    b. Free counterpoint: voices unrelated, nonimitative counterpoint.

    c. Imitative counterpoint: voices share same thematic material.

    d. All voices are similar in importance.

    e. One voice is in long notes (probably a borrowed tune, or *cantus firmus*) whereas the others are in faster figurations. In which voice is the *cantus firmus?*

    f. If there is a *cantus firmus,* are the other voices imitative or free?

2. Harmony.

  a) The harmonic phrase in example 4.3 is a prolongation of I. Analyze with RNs (Roman numerals) (notice that the first inversion of V_7 is labeled V^6_5, a chord very similar to V_6), and explain the prolongation of I in terms of voice leading. Show the linear voice-leading structure of these measures in the staves below (piano accompaniment only) using a reductive notation modeled after example 4.7b in the book.

Example 4.3a   Felix Mendelssohn, "Im Grünen," from *Zwölf Gesänge,* op. 8, no. 11, mm. 14–15

Will kom - men im Grü - nen! Der Him - mel ist blau, der

Example 4.3b

b) Analyze mm. 15–16 and 18–19 of example 4.4 with RNs. Measure 15, beats 1–2, presents an incomplete chord, which could be read as an A or an F chord if we imply the missing pitch. If we consider the F chord in beats 3–4, and by analogy with m. 16 (all of it is one chord), we will hear the complete m. 15 as an F chord. The symbol V^{6-5}_{4-3}, which will be explained in chapters 5 and 9, should be interpreted as a dominant chord (the $\frac{5}{3}$) embellished melodically by the preceding $^6_4$ (which we call a "cadential $^6_4$").

1) What is the role of first-inversion chords in this passage? Mark all changes of position with a bracket, and explain them.

FM:

Gm:

R:

KEYBOARD PROGRESSIONS   Play the following progressions in CM, GM, DM, and FM; and in Cm, Gm, Dm, and Am. You can also use them to practice harmonic dictation. A friend can play them in any order, while you notate the bass and Roman numerals and recognize which one of the progressions is being played.

♪♪ Example 4.5

Chapter 5

Cadences

EXERCISE 5.1 *Analysis.* Study and label each of the following cadences. Name the cadence type, and list specific RNs (Roman numerals) and other characteristics to justify your choice.

1. Anthology, no. 52, Verdi, *La traviata*:
   Measures 31–32:

   Measures 41–42:

2. Anthology, no. 19, Haydn, Minuet, m. 8.

3. Anthology, no. 31, Paradis, *Sicilienne*:
   Measures 3–4:

   Measures 27–28:

4. Anthology, no. 28, Mozart, Piano Sonata in B♭M, III, m. 76.

5. Example 5.1.

6. Example 5.2.

7. Example 5.3.
   Measures 19–20:

   Measures 20–22:

8. Example 5.4.

Example 5.1   George Frideric Handel, "Hallelujah," from *Messiah,* Closing Measures

Example 5.2   J. S. Bach, Chorale 143, *In dulci jubilo,* mm. 20–24

Example 5.3   Robert Schumann, "Ich will meine Seele tauchen," from *Dichterliebe*, op. 48, no. 5

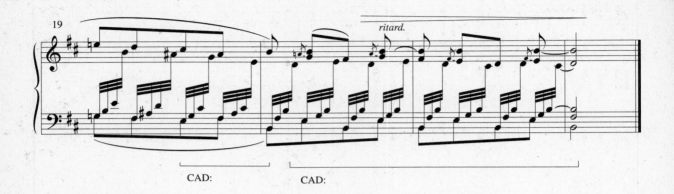

Example 5.4   J. S. Bach, Invention no. 4 in Dm, mm. 46–52

EXERCISE 5.2   Realize the following cadences in four voices as required. Some soprano melodic patterns are provided, and so are some Roman numerals. Provide RNs where missing.

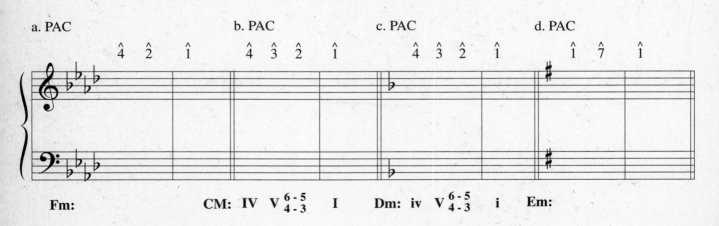

e. IAC   f. IAC   g. IAC   h. HC

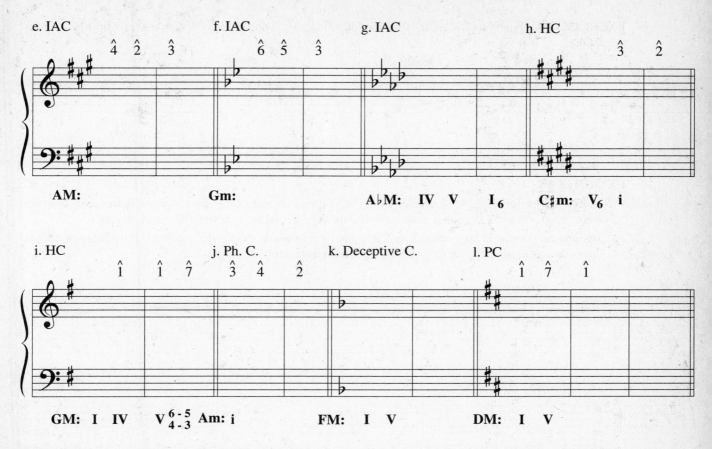

AM: Gm: A♭M: IV V   I₆   C♯m: V₆ i

i. HC   j. Ph. C.   k. Deceptive C.   l. PC

GM: I IV   V $^{6\text{ - }5}_{4\text{ - }3}$ Am: i   FM: I V   DM: I V

EXERCISE 5.3   Complete the following figured bass progressions in four voices, after analyzing each of them with RNs. Name the cadence type in each case.

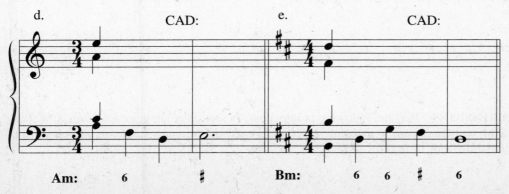

a.   CAD: b.   CAD: c.   CAD:

DM: 6   GM: 6   Dm: 6   6   ♯

d.   CAD: e.   CAD:

Am: 6   ♯   Bm: 6   6   ♯   6

EXERCISE 5.4 Provide a RN analysis for the following bass, using only I, IV, and V in root position and first inversion.

AM:

EXERCISE 5.5

1. Harmonize exercise 5.5a in four voices (bass, RNs, inner voices). Name the cadences. Remember: what you are writing *is music*. Listen to it, make sure it sounds good, and enjoy *both* writing and playing it.

2. Harmonize exercise 5.5b with bass and RNs (no inner voices). Name the cadences. Remember to double-check this outer-voice frame for good first-species counterpoint.

KEYBOARD PROGRESSIONS Play the following progressions, in the following keys: CM, Am, GM, Em, DM, Bm, FM, Dm, BbM, and Gm. Learn to recognize the various cadential formulas aurally as you play them, and do aural recognition drills with a friend.

♪♪ Example 5.5

Chapter 6

Melodic Organization I: Phrase Structure

EXERCISE 6.1 *Analysis.* Study the phrase/period structure of the following examples. For each of the examples, provide a brief discussion of structure, including at least the following information:

1. Is the fragment based on a motive?

2. How many phrases are there? Provide measure numbers and phrase numbers for each. Are any phrases connected by elision?

3. Identify the cadences at the end of each phrase. In cases where only a melody is given, you can identify cadences on the basis of the given Roman numerals and the cadential melodic gestures.

4. Is there any antecedent-consequent phrase structure?

5. What kind of a period is this? One or several of the following may apply to each example: parallel, contrasting, symmetrical, asymmetrical, three-phrase (or four-phrase), double, modulating, phrase group (not a period).

6. Provide a line (bubble) diagram for each of the examples, indicating the following items: phrases/measure numbers; phrase relationship with letters; cadences at the end of each phrase (with a cadence-type abbreviation); and long-range harmonic motion from beginning to end of each phrase.

Examples for analysis:

1. Anthology, no. 22, Chevalier de Saint–Georges, Violin Concerto.

   Discussion:

   Form diagram:

2. Anthology, no. 6, Minuet from *Notebook for Anna Magdalena Bach,* mm.1–16.

   Discussion:

   Form diagram:

---

3. Example 6.1.

   Discussion:

   Form diagram:

Example 6.1   Amy Beach, *Sweetheart, Sigh No More,* op. 14, no. 3, mm. 3–13

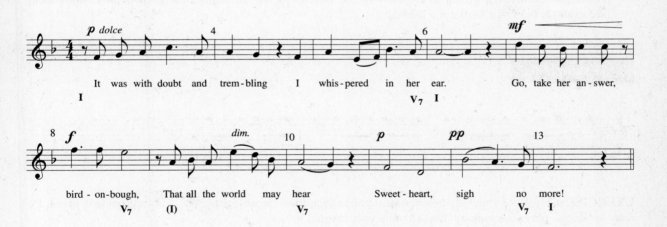

4. Anthology, no. 32, Beethoven, Piano Sonata in Fm, op. 2, no.1, III, Menuetto, mm. 1–14.

   Discussion:

   Form diagram:

5. Anthology, no. 32, Beethoven, Piano Sonata in Fm, op. 2, no.1, III, Trio, mm. 41–50

Discussion:

Form diagram:

---

6. Notate (rhythm only) the most characteristic melodic rhythmic motive in:
   a) Anthology, no. 6, Minuet from *Notebook for A. M. Bach.*

   b) Anthology, no. 19, Haydn, Minuet.

   c) Anthology, no. 26, Mozart, Piano Sonata in CM, III.

7. In anthology, no. 19 (Haydn, Minuet), the combination of rhythmic motive, phrasing, and harmonic resolution create a series of elisions in mm. 1–4. Given the rhythm of these measures in example 6.2, show the phrasing of the motives with brackets (there will be three of them), indicating clearly where the elisions occur (see example 6.3 in the book for a model).

Example 6.2

EXERCISE 6.2   Write a melody in antecedent-consequent form (a parallel period). The beginning is given. Be ready to sing or play your melody if asked to by your instructor.

EXERCISE 6.3   Write a melody with the following characteristics: four phrases (double period), form $a_1-b_1-a_2-b_2$, sixteen measures long. Indicate what cadences are implied at the end of each phrase. Be musical, and be able to sing what you write.

EM:

EXERCISE 6.4   Analyze the following progression with RNs, and realize in four voices.

Gm: 6   6   #   6   #   6   ♮

EXERCISE 6.5 Harmonize the following melody with a bass and RNs, a chord per note. Use only i, iv, and V in root position or first inversion (for notes indicated with a 6). Label the cadences at the end of each phrase. Remember to double-check this outer-voice frame for good first-species counterpoint.

well-organized, analytical paper. Turn in an annotated copy of the score, on which you will mark the following information, which you should also cover in your paper:

a) Circle the main motive of the piece.

b) Are there any prominent rhythmic motives in this fragment? What are they?

c) Mark with brackets (one per segment) all the sequences in the piece.

d) Label and number the phrases (phrase 1, phrase 2, etc.).

e) Are the two phrase members of phrase 1 (mm. 1–4) similar or contrasting?

f) How many periods are there?

g) Mark and label all the cadences in the piece.

h) Could the piece have ended in m. 16?

i) What is the formal function of mm. 17–18?

j) Provide a line diagram of the complete piece, indicating phrases, periods, cadences (with abbreviations and RNs), measure numbers, and letters to indicate form.

11. Discuss the techniques of thematic (melodic) development in anthology, no. 32, Beethoven, op. 2, no. 1, I, mm. 1–20. Notice specifically the following relationships, and provide exact terms:

a) Measures 1–2 with 3–4:

b) Measures 5–6 with 1–2:

c) Measure 6 with m. 5:

d) Measures 11–14 with 1–2:

e) Measures 15–16 and following (to m. 20):

EXERCISE 7.2   Write extended or varied versions of the following melody using the devices specified in each case. Be austere in your versions (do not try to vary or add too much; only what is necessary to make good musical sense). Make sure that your versions are musical, and that you are satisfied with them.

a. Repetition

b. Variation (rhythmic, or pitch and rhythm)

c. Sequence

d. Change of mode

e. Interpolation by fragmentation

f. Intervallic expansion or contraction

g. Cadential extension

h. Augmentation

i. Inversion (begin on pitch B)

j. Retrograde

EXERCISE 7.3

1. Complete the following parallel period with a consequent.

2. After you write your consequent, and using your own music paper, write four more versions of the same consequent, using the following extensions in each of them. Think musically, and write extension that you think make good musical sense in the context of this period.

   a) An interpolation using fragmentation and sequence.

   b) An interpolation using repetition and variation.

   c) An interpolation using new melodic material.

   d) A cadential extension.

EXERCISE 7.4   Provide a RN analysis and realize in four voices.

Chapter 8

Nonchord Tones

EXERCISE 8.1   Analysis.

1. Identify and label all NCTs (nonchord tones) in the Corelli phrase reproduced in example 8.1. Besides the NCTs actually present in the melody, is any other NCT suggested by the figured bass?

2. Identify and label all the NCTs in anthology, no. 8 (Bach, Chorale 41), mm. 1–5.

3. Identify and label all the NCTs in anthology, no. 34 (Beethoven, Piano Sonata in Cm, op. 13, III), mm. 1–8. Because in this example the left hand arpeggiates chords, all the left-hand pitches may be interpreted as chord tones, with the only exceptions to be found in m. 1, beat 2 (notice the meter signature), and m. 3, beat 2. Identify the NCTs in these left-hand passages, besides the numerous NCTs throughout the right-hand melody.

♪♪♪ **Example 8.1**   Archangelo Corelli, Sonata *La Folia*, op. 5, no. 12

EXERCISE 8.2   Add NCTs to the following chorale. Provide suspensions as required by the given figures. If you add simultaneous NCTs in different voices, make sure they are consonant among themselves. Be careful not to "overembellish"!

b.

E♭M:
HR:

Germany

Chapter 9

$^6_4$ Chords

EXERCISE 9.1   Analysis.

1. Circle and identify the $^6_4$ chord(s) in the following excerpt. Notice that the double bass sounds an octave lower than notated.

Example 9.1   L. v. Beethoven, Piano Concerto no. 1, op. 15, I, mm. 1–8

2. Refer to anthology, no. 22 (Chevalier de Saint–Georges, Violin Concerto, no.1). Turn in a copy of the excerpt, in which you will have circled, identified, and labeled the following:

   a) all $^6_4$ chords.

   b) all NCTs (nonchord tones) in the first violin melody.

3. Circle and label the $^6_4$ chords in the following excerpt.

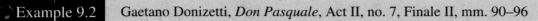

Example 9.2   Gaetano Donizetti, *Don Pasquale*, Act II, no. 7, Finale II, mm. 90–96

4. a) Identify and name the type of period in example 9.3.

    b) What NCT is featured in the opening motive?

    c) Measures 5–6 are linear elaborations of the tonic triad. On the score, provide RNs for all the chords in these two measures. Explain here how each of the chords functions linearly to prolong the tonic harmony. How are the outer-voice pitches in m. 5 related linearly?

    d) What kind of cadence closes the first phrase (m. 8)?

        What kind of cadence closes the period?

        Explain the chords in mm. 15–16.

    e) How are the two "moving voices" in both hands related in mm. 1–4?
        By contrast, compare the *outer* voices in mm. 5–6. How is the contour of these voices designed in relation with each other?

        Finally, compare the contrapuntal motion in both hands in mm. 7–8. How are the melodic contours related in these measures?

Example 9.3   L. v. Beethoven, Piano Sonata no. 9, op. 14, no. I, II, mm. 1–16

EXERCISE 9.4   Realize the following progression in four voices. Provide RNs where needed. Remember to double-check the outer-voice frame for good first-species counterpoint.

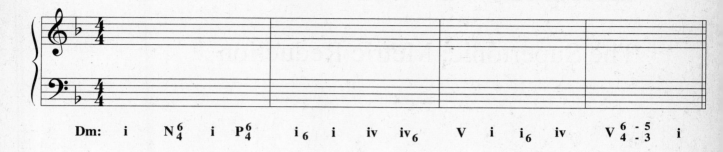

Dm: i   N$^6_4$ i   P$^6_4$ i$_6$ i   iv   iv$_6$ V   i   i$_6$ iv   V$^{6-5}_{4-3}$ i

EXERCISE 9.5   Harmonize the following melody with a bass line and RNs (no inner voices), using only i, iv, V, and their inversions. Use a passing $^6_4$ and a cadential $^6_4$ in places where the melody allows for them. In the measures marked with brackets under the harmonic rhythm, use a change of chord position to keep the bass moving. Write as many voice exchanges as possible. Remember to double-check this outer-voice frame for good first-species counterpoint.

F♯m:
HR:

KEYBOARD PROGRESSIONS   The following keyboard progressions contain all of the $^6_4$ chord types studied in this chapter. Play and learn the progressions in CM, FM, B♭M, E♭M, and in their relative minor keys: Am, Dm, Gm, and Cm.

Example 9.5   J. S. Bach, Brandenburg Concerto no. 6, III, mm. 1–8

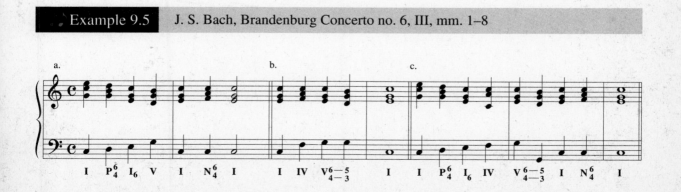

a.   b.   c.

I   P$^6_4$ I$_6$ V   I   N$^6_4$ I   I   IV   V$^{6-5}_{4-3}$ I   I   P$^6_4$ I$_6$ IV   V$^{6-5}_{4-3}$ I   N$^6_4$ I

Chapter 10

The Supertonic; Metric Reduction

EXERCISE 10.1 Analysis.

1. Analyze the opening phrase of Beethoven's Piano Concerto no. 4, III (example 10.1) with Roman numerals (RNs). What is the harmonic function of mm. 11–15? How does this phrase illustrate the close relationship between ii and IV?

Example 10.1 L. v. Beethoven, Piano Concerto no. 4, op. 58, III, mm. 11–20 (Piano Part)

KEYBOARD PROGRESSIONS   Play and learn the progressions in example 10.2 (in CM, DM, AM, and E♭M; play progressions 10.2d and e also in Am, Bm, F#m, and Cm), paying attention to the voice leading to and from the supertonic chords. Listen carefully to the progressions as you play them (or as a classmate plays them).

♪♪ Example 10.2

Chapter 11

Harmonic Rhythm; Hypermeter

EXERCISE 11.1   Analysis.

1. In the spaces below, diagram the harmonic rhythm (HR) for each of the following examples. For each of these examples, indicate also whether the HR is very slow, slow, fast, regular, irregular, and/or accelerating toward a cadence.

   a) Anthology, no. 26, Mozart, Piano Sonata in CM, K. 309, III, mm. 1–19.

   b) Anthology, no. 32, Beethoven, Piano Sonata in Fm, op. 2, no. 1, I, mm. 1–20.

   c) Anthology, no. 32, Beethoven, Piano Sonata in Fm, op. 2, no. 1, I, mm.140–152.

   d) Anthology, no. 33, Beethoven, Piano Sonata in Cm, op. 10, no. 1, II, mm. 1–8.

2. *Metric and harmonic accents.* Provide diagrams of HR along with symbols of strong and weak metric accent for each of the following examples. Discuss briefly how metric and harmonic accents correlate. How are V and I chords placed metrically? Is there any clear conflict between metric and harmonic accents?

   a) Anthology, no. 50, Schumann, "Folk Song".

b) Anthology, no. 33, Beethoven, Piano Sonata in Cm, op. 10, no. 1, II, mm. 1–8.

3. Provide diagrams similar to example 11.11 in the textbook for the following examples. Add arrows over the graph to show structural accents. Show the strong or weak hypermetric role of complete measures (or, in the case of Beethoven's op. 2, no.1, of two-bar hypermeasures), and discuss briefly the metric accent/tonal accent relationships, noting especially the metric placement of I and V chords.

a) Anthology, no. 28, Mozart, Piano Sonata in B♭M, K. 333, III, mm. 9–16.

b) Anthology, no. 34, Beethoven, Piano Sonata in Cm, op. 13, III, mm. 1–8.

c) Anthology, no. 32, Beethoven, Piano Sonata in Fm, op. 2, no. 1, I, mm. 1–8.

4. Analyze example 11.1 with Roman numerals (RNs), and provide weak/strong metric symbols above each beat in the score. Then, discuss briefly in the space below the relationship between metric and harmonic accents, focusing on metric placement for the different harmonic functions and for the chord successions implying a tension-release progression.

Example 11.1   J. S. Bach, Chorale 22, "Schmücke dich, o liebe Seele," mm. 1–5

EXERCISE 11.2   *Writing harmonic progressions.* Be careful with the correlation of metric and harmonic accents, and write harmonic phrases that are logical and musical. Play your progressions and make sure you like them!

1. Write a progression (bass and RNs only) in DM, in $\frac{4}{4}$, using only I, IV, and V, and their first inversions.

DM:

2. Write a progression in B♭M, in $\frac{3}{4}$, using only I, IV, and V, ii, and their first inversions.

B♭M:

3. Write a progression in Fm, in $\frac{2}{4}$, including a deceptive resolution of V, a cadential $^6_4$, and a plagal cadence.

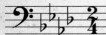

Fm:

4. Write a progression in Bm, in $\frac{6}{8}$, using a passing $^6_4$, a neighbor $^6_4$, and a cadential $^6_4$, besides i, iv, V, and ii in root position or inversion.

Bm:

EXERCISE 11.3   Harmonize the following melodies with RNs and write a keyboard realization of your harmonization. You should begin by determining the correct HR for each melody, taking into account any possible NCTs (nonchord tones). Use only the chords we have studied so far. Find places where you can possibly use the supertonic chord and any of the $^6_4$ chords we have studied.

a.   **Moderato**

Cm:

b.   **Allegro vivo**   Britain

DM:

Chapter 12

The Dominant Seventh and Its Inversions

EXERCISE 12.1 *Analysis.* Refer to anthology, no. 20, Haydn, Sonata in DM.

1. Analyze mm. 9–15 with RNs (Roman numerals).

2. Measures 9–15 can be explained as a harmonic prolongation of I in FM. Explain the linear function of each chord and how it contributes to this extended prolongation.

3. Provide a prolongational reduction of the left hand for this passage, indicating graphically the linear functions of each pitch. Refer to examples 12.6e, 12.8b, and 12.10b in the textbook for notational models.

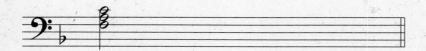

4. Provide RNs for the chords in mm. 17–19. Explain their voice leading, noticing the resolution of any possible chordal dissonance.

DM:
HR:

Italy

KEYBOARD PROGRESSIONS   Practice the keyboard progressions from example 12.1 in the following major keys: C, G, D, A, E, F, B♭, and A♭; and in the following minor keys: A, D, G, C, F, E, B, and F♯.

Example 12.1

Chapter 13

The Leading-Tone Triad

EXERCISE 13.1   Analysis.

1. a) Identify a leading-tone triad in each of the following examples: anthology, no. 20 (Haydn, Piano Sonata in DM), mm. 1–4; and anthology, no. 32 (Beethoven, Piano Sonata in Fm, op. 2, no. 1), mm. 1–8. Explain how each of these triads functions linearly, and comment on the voice leading used in their resolution.

   b) How is the initial tonic in the Beethoven example prolonged through m. 7? Fill in, in the staff below, the harmonies that prolong i between m. 2 and m. 7, showing graphically their linear nature. Notice the notation of the last two chords as provided, which indicates the role of V as a goal (a cadence) in this phrase, and the subordinate, predominant role of ii°₆.

i   ii°₆   V

2. Analyze example 13.1 with RNs (Roman numerals). There are two areas that extend I: mm. 21–23 prolong I and lead to the half cadence at m. 24. Then, mm. 25–30 again prolong I, leading to the final predominant-dominant-tonic cadential pattern. Provide a prolongational reduction of the complete chorale in the staves

below, showing the linear function of the chords within these two areas. Make sure you indicate all the neighbor (N) and passing (P) functions of these chords. A reduction of the bass for the first phrase is provided as a model.

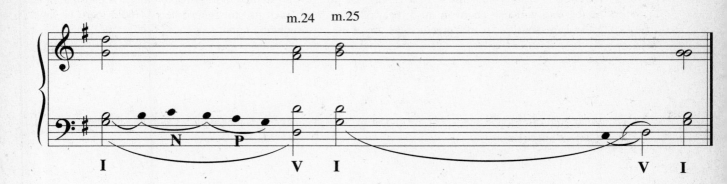

Example 13.1   R. Schumann, "Freue dich, o meine Seele," from *Album for the Young,* op. 68, mm. 21–32.

3. Example 13.2 shows mm. 3–6 of Bach's Chorale 96.

   a) Analyze mm. 3–4 with RNs.

   b) Circle and label all NCTs (nonchord tones).

   c) Measure 3, beats 3–4 and m. 4, beat 1, feature a progression studied in this chapter. What is unusual, in a minor key, with the chord in m. 3, beat 3? Why does Bach use this chord here? Could there be any melodic reasons that would preclude the use of the corresponding minor key chord?

   d) What kind of cadence appears at the end of m. 4? (Consider the cadential chord and the one that precedes it before answering.)

♪ Example 13.2   J. S. Bach, Chorale 96, "Jesu, meine Freude," mm. 3–6

EXERCISE 13.2   Analyze the following figured bass with RNs, and realize it in four voices. End the phrase with a $\hat{5}$–#$\hat{6}$–#$\hat{7}$–$\hat{1}$ melodic fragment in the soprano. Remember to double-check your outer-voice frame for good first-species counterpoint.

EXERCISE 13.3   Harmonize each of the following short melodic fragments in four voices. Write the bass and RNs first, then fill in the inner voices. Use leading-tone triads for the notes marked with an asterisk.

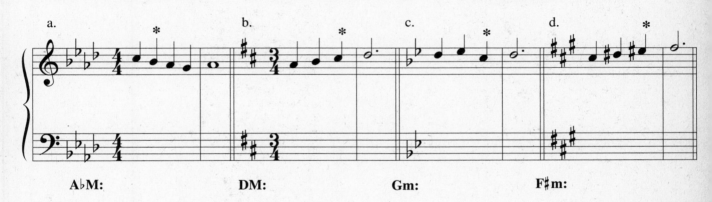

EXERCISE 13.4   Harmonize the following melody in four voices, with a correct chordal progression and good voice leading. Harmonize all the soprano pitches as chord tones. Three of the pitches may be harmonized with vii°$_6$, and for the rest you may use I, IV, ii, or V$_7$ in root position or inversion. Remember to double-check your outer-voice frame for good first-species counterpoint.

KEYBOARD PROGRESSIONS   Play the keyboard progressions in example 13.3 in a variety of keys as assigned by your instructor. Notice that example 13.3c can only be played in M if you wish to avoid the ♭$\hat{6}$–♯$\hat{7}$ augmented 2nd. Example 13.3d provides a version of the same progression with $\hat{6}$ and $\hat{7}$ in different voices, suitable to be played in both M and m.

Example 13.3

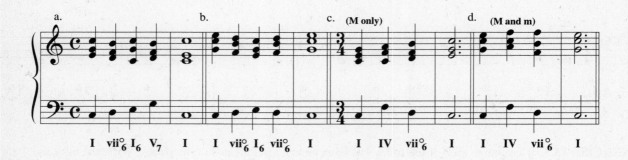

a. I vii°$_6$ I$_6$ V$_7$ I   b. I vii°$_6$ I$_6$ vii°$_6$ I   c. (M only) I IV vii°$_6$ I   d. (M and m) I IV vii°$_6$ I

Chapter 14

The Mediant, Submediant, and Subtonic Triads; Diatonic Sequences

EXERCISE 14.1   Analysis.

1. The cadence marked with a bracket in example 14.1 appears to be a PAC (perfect authentic cadence) in Bm. Examine it closely, and comment on the exact type of cadence this is, and on the chords involved in it.

♪♪ Example 14.1   J. S. Bach, Air, from Orchestral Suite no. 3, BWV 1068, m. 10

Bm:

2. a) How is I in CM prolonged in mm. 41–43 of example 14.2? Explain exactly what chords are used by Brahms in these measures, and how they function. Do you see any instance of 5–6 technique?

   b) In m. 44 the bass seems to indicate a dominant harmony. Is the chord throughout the measure a plain V, or is the dominant harmony elaborated in any way?

   c) This passage is in ⁶⁄₈. How does Brahms alter your perception of this meter? What metric ambiguities can you identify, considering phrasing, rhythmic accents, and grouping?

♪ Example 14.2   Johannes Brahms, Intermezzo in CM, op. 119, no. 3, mm. 41–45

3. a) Analyze mm. 1–4 of anthology, no. 24 (Mozart, DM Sonata) with RNs (Roman numerals). What is the function of vi in this phrase?

b) Analyze mm. 9–12 of anthology, no. 28 (Mozart, B♭M Sonata) with RNs. What is the function of vi in this phrase? How does the harmonization of this phrase compare with the one you just analyzed in the DM Sonata? What kind of NCTs (nonchord tones) are featured in m. 11?

c) Refer to anthology, no. 19 (Haydn, Divertimento in CM, Trio), and explain the resolution of the dominant of E♭M in mm. 31–32.

4. a) Analyze mm. 1–10 in example 14.3 with RNs.

Questions b to h refer to mm. 1–10.

b) vi is used to prolong the tonic twice in this passage. In what measures?

c) How is the dominant prolonged linearly in m. 7? How is it resolved to m. 8 and why?

d) This passage is mainly harmonized using descending 5th root motions. Mark every root progression of 5th in the example with brackets. (Notice that some of these root progressions appear in first inversion. Mark them anyway.)

e) This passage is based on two melodic motives. Circle each appearance of either motive, and label them with a 1 or a 2. How is each of these motives characteristic (and immediately recognizable), and how do they contrast from one another?

f) Do the motives appear in literal transpositions every time they are repeated, or are they varied somehow? How?

g) Are mm. 8–9 related to any of the two motives? How?

h) Describe the texture in mm. 1–10. What is the role of each line?

i) How does the texture and the roles of instruments change in mm. 11–25?

j) How is motive 2 treated in mm. 15–17? Be very specific, and circle in these measures the pitches from the original motives in mm. 5–7.

k) On what kind of cadence does the passage close?

l) What is the function of the bass in mm. 20–25? Use the exact term (which you learned in chapter 8).

Example 14.3   L. v. Beethoven, Sonata for Violin and Piano, op. 24 (*Spring*), I, mm. 1–25

Example 14.3   Continued

5. a) Analyze and compare the three phrases in example 14.4. Refer back to example 10.7 in the textbook (Bach's "Chaconne" for violin) and read the commentary after that example. Now consider the bass in the three phrases of example 14.4 (in examples 14.4a and b, consider only the downbeat of each measure). What kind of bass is this? How is this piece similar to the Bach fragment in example 10.7?

    b) What is the common underlying progression in both examples 14.4a and b (consider chord roots)? What is the compositional principle (the element of formal growth) in all three phrases?

    c) Compare example 14.4a to the paradigms in example 14.13 in the textbook. Can you see any voice-leading relationships between this phrase and one or more of the paradigms?

        Now do the same comparison for example 14.4b.

        Finally, what basic harmonic/voice-leading technique can you identify in example 14.4c? Consider only the left hand, and you will find two separate and familiar voice-leading patterns, one of them taking into account the second eighth note in each measure and its motion to the half note, and the other one considering the suspension figure and its resolution to the half note.

♪♪ Example 14.4   G. F. Handel, "Chaconne," from *Trois Leçons,* mm. 89–92, 105–109, and 113–117

EXERCISE 14.2   Analyze the following figured bass with RNs, and realize it in four voices.

EXERCISE 14.3

1. Write a complete circle of 5ths in four voices.

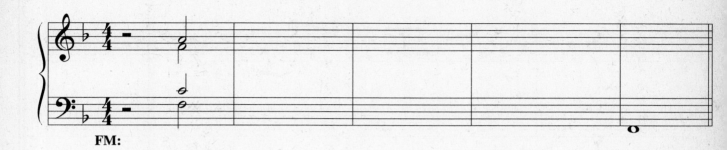

FM:

2. Realize the progression in four voices. Notice that it combines three sequential paradigms we have studied in this chapter. Realize the sequences following your models in the textbook (examples 14.13 and 14.15), and be very careful with doublings and faulty parallel 8ves or 5ths.

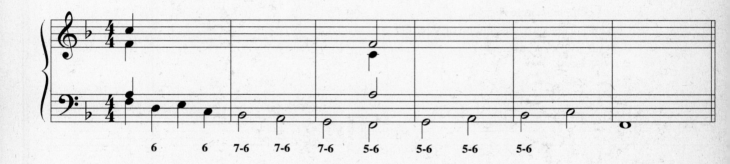

EXERCISE 14.4   Provide a RN analysis for the following bass line, treating each pitch as a chord tone.

EXERCISE 14.5   Harmonize the following melody with a bass line and RNs, using the given HR (harmonic rhythm). Include the following chords in your harmonization: III, vii°₆, a deceptive resolution of V, a cadential $^6_4$, and a plagal cadence at the end.

EXERCISE 14.6

1. Write progressions (bass and RNs) using the chords indicated in each case, in the required meters.

    a) A complete circle of 5ths.

    b) vii°₆, a deceptive resolution of V.

    c) VII, III, V$^4_2$, a cadential $^6_4$.

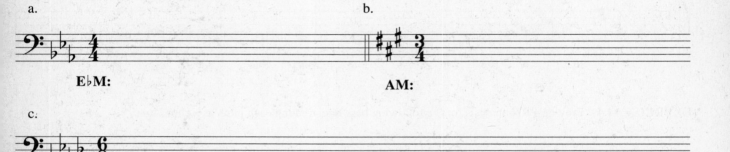

2. Choose one of your own progressions from above, and use it as a harmonic basis to compose a phrase for a melodic instrument of your choice (such as flute, clarinet in B♭, violin, etc.) and keyboard accompaniment. Your phrase should consist of a simple melody (for the melodic instrument) with a keyboard-style accompaniment (both hands).

EXERCISE 14.7   On your own music paper, realize the following harmonic sequences in four voices (two $^4_4$ measures each).

1. A root-position circle of 5ths with a 10–10–10–10 outer-voice paradigm, in Cm.

2. A circle of 5ths alternating root-position and first-inversion chords, with a 10–6–10–6 outer-voice paradigm, in GM.

3. A sequence descending by steps using the 7–6 technique, in CM.

4. A sequence by descending 3rds with interpolated $^5_3$ chords (with a bass pattern down a 4th, up a step), in Bm.

KEYBOARD PROGRESSIONS

1. Play the keyboard progression in example 14.5 in the keys assigned by your instructor. (Suggested keys: CM, AM, EM, E♭M, A♭M; and Am, F♯m, C♯m, Cm, and Fm.)

2. Play all the sequential paradigms from examples 14.13, 14.15, and 14.18 in the textbook, if possible in several keys besides AM (for instance, CM and GM).

♩♩ Example 14.5

Chapter 15

Other Diatonic Seventh Chords

EXERCISE 15.1   Analysis.

1. Study mm. 1–12 of anthology, no. 47, Schumann, "Ich grolle nicht."

   a) Provide RNs (Roman numerals) for mm. 1–9. Notice that the first chord in m. 3, which we studied in this chapter, actually belongs to Cm because of the A♭ (♭$\hat{6}$). Assign it the same RN you would in Cm, and think of it as a chord "borrowed" from the minor mode. Do not assign a RN to the second chord in m. 4, but rather explain how it functions linearly.

   b) What is the underlying progression (think of downbeat chords for each measure) in mm. 4–9? Think of both root progression and chordal progression. Then, how do the "upbeat" chords in each measure function?

   c) Think of mm. 9–12 as an extended V_7–I progression. How are the V_7 at m. 9 and the I at m. 12 connected linearly? Think first of the bass motion from $\hat{5}$ to $\hat{1}$. And then look also at the piano's top voice, moving down from $\hat{2}$ to $\hat{3}$. How would the term "wedge" apply to this contrapuntal gesture?

   d) 1) In which ways is the melody unified (motivically? rhythmically? other?)?

2) The words mean: "I hold no resentment, and even if my heart breaks, O love forever lost, I hold no resentment." How is the heartbreak ("Herz") expressed and intensified musically?

How is the concept of love lost (and the subsequent feeling of grief) expressed (think, for instance, of the bass line on the words "ewig verlornes Lieb," but also of how the singer expresses the loss: Where is the climactic high point of the fragment?)?

What bass motion accompanies the final two statements of "ich grolle nicht"? If this contour, as opposed to the bass line in mm. 4–9, shows some hope, is the feeling confirmed by the lines in both the voice and the piano's right hand in mm. 9–12?

2. a) Examine mm. 25–26 of example 15.1. What is the type of progression? What kind of voice-leading paradigm do you recognize (refer to the paradigms studied in chapter 14)?

   b) Compare mm. 25–26 with 30–32. How is the latter progression different than the former? Analyze the chords and voice leading in mm. 30–32 carefully.

   c) The passage closes with a cadential pedal on $\hat{1}$ prolonging a I chord (mm. 32–36). Assume for now that all of m.32 is a I chord, with a prolonging passing-tone F on beat 2. What are the other two chords used on the pedal (mm. 33 and 35)?

3. How does Paradis prolong the tonic in mm. 6–8 of example 15.2? What standard cadential formula (including the predominant chord—do not overlook the vocal line) does she use?

♪♪ Example 15.1   J. Brahms, Ballade, op. 118, no. 3, mm. 23–36.

EXERCISE 15.4   Harmonize the following melody with a keyboard texture. Include two leading-tone seventh chords, a deceptive progression, and a cadential 4–3 suspension.

FM:

HR:

EXERCISE 15.5

1. Write a diatonic seventh circle of 5ths in four voices.

Dm:

2. Write a second version of this progression for piano, and compose a melody on it.

KEYBOARD PROGRESSIONS Play the progressions in example 15.3 in a variety of M and m keys, as assigned by your instructor. (Suggested keys: CM, GM, DM, AM, EM, FM, B♭M, E♭M, A♭M, and their relative minor keys.)

♪ Example 15.3

PART 2

*Chromatic Harmony
and Form*

Chapter 16

Secondary Dominants I

EXERCISE 16.1   Analysis.

1. Refer to anthology, no. 34 (Beethoven, Sonata in Cm, op. 13, III), mm. 12–16. What chord is tonicized twice in these measures? Provide a RN (Roman numeral) analysis for this complete passage.

2. What secondary dominant can you identify in example 16.1, m. 18, beat 4? And in m. 20, beat 1? Provide exact RNs for each.

| Example 16.1 | J. S. Bach, Chorale 107, "Herzlich lieb hab'ich dich, o Herr," mm. 16–21 |

3. Example 16.2 presents a clear prolongation of the tonic chord. Explain. How is it prolonged? Are chromaticism or tonicization part of this prolongation? Which degree is tonicized, and how?

Example 16.2   W. A. Mozart, Piano Quartet in E♭M, K. 493, I, mm. 1–5

4. Example 16.3 begins with a secondary dominant. Provide RNs for the complete example. Does it feature any other tonicization? When is the tonic clearly established?

Example 16.3   L. v. Beethoven, Symphony no. 1 in CM, op. 21, I, mm. 1–6

EXERCISE 16.2   Write and resolve the following secondary dominant chords. The resolution should be to the appropriate tonicized chord, in root position or inversion as required by the voice leading in the bass.

Em: V_7/V ____   Dm: V_7/iv ____   FM: V_5^6/IV ____   GM: V_3^4/V ____   AM: V_2^4/V ____   Cm: V_5^6/iv ____

E♭M: V_2^4/IV ____   F♯m: V_3^4/iv ____   Gm: V_5^6/V ____   B♭M: V_7/IV ____   Fm: V_2^4/iv ____   BM: V_7/V ____

EXERCISE 16.3   Realize the following short progressions in four voices. Check the outer-voice frame for good counterpoint.

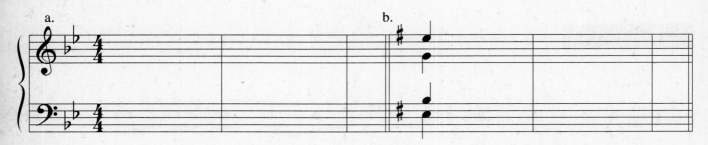

B♭M: I   IV V_7/V V   vi V_5^6/IV IV V_7 I   Em: i V_2^4/iv iv$_6$ V_7 i V_2^4/V V$_6$ V_7 i

EXERCISE 16.4   Analyze the following progression with RNs, and realize it in four voices.

EXERCISE 16.5

1. Harmonize the following melody with a bass and RNs or a figured bass, according to the suggested harmonic rhythm. Include a tonicization of iv and one of V.

2. Once you are sure that your harmonization is correct, copy the melody again on your own music paper and, below it, provide a left-hand keyboard realization of your harmonization.

EXERCISE 16.6

1. Write your own progressions (bass and RNs) in the keys and meters indicated below. Use the required chords, besides any of the other chords we have already studied. Make sure you resolve secondary dominants (and any other chords that require resolution) correctly.

   a) F♯m; include V_2^4/iv, $ii^{\varnothing 6}_5$, V_5^6/V, and a cad. $^6_4$.

   b) GM; include V_7/IV and V_3^4/V.

a.

F♯m:

b.

GM:

2. Choose one of your own progressions from above, and use it as a harmonic basis to compose a phrase for a melodic instrument and keyboard accompaniment.

KEYBOARD PROGRESSIONS   Play the keyboard progressions in Example 16.4 in the keys assigned by your instructor. (Suggested keys: CM, Cm, GM, Gm, DM, Dm, FM, Fm, B♭M, B♭m, D♭M, C♯m.)

♩) Example 16.4

Chapter 17

Secondary Dominants II

EXERCISE 17.1 Analysis.

1. Refer back to example 16.1 (Bach, Chorale 107). We have already identified tonicizations of IV and V in the last phrase of this example. What degree is tonicized at the end of the first phrase (m. 16, fermata)? And what other degree is immediately tonicized at the beginning of the second phrase (m. 16, beat 4 to m. 17, beat 1)? Provide RNs (Roman numerals) for both tonicizations.

2. Provide RNs for the tonicization in mm. 2–3 of example 17.1.

♪ Example 17.1   Anton Bruckner, Symphony no. 7, II, mm. 1–4

3. Identify, with exact RNs, the tonicizations in the following spots of example 17.2:

  a) Measure 2 (to the fermata).

  b) Measure 3, beats 1–2.

  c) Measures 5–6.

  d) Measure 8 (to the fermata).

The phrase in m. 8, beat 4 to m. 10, beat 1, constitutes a secondary key area. What degree is tonicized? Analyze this phrase with RNs using secondary key area notation.

Example 17.2   J. S. Bach, Chorale 20, "Ein' feste Burg ist unser Gott"

4. Refer to anthology, no. 5 (Vivaldi, Concerto in GM, op. 3, no. 3). Analyze, and provide RNs for, the following tonicizations:

   a) Measures 7–10.

   b) Measures 11–15 (analyze these measures as a secondary key area).

   c) Measures 17–18.

   d) Measures 19–20.

   e) Measures 26–27.

5. Analyze example 17.3. What progression is it based on? What kind of chords is this progression built on? Can you comment on some special voice-leading properties we studied in this chapter?

6. Analyze example 17.4.

   a) What compositional principle are mm. 14–17 based on? (That is, how are the pairs of measures related?)

   b) Measures 18–21 are also based on the same principle.

      1) Comment on the melodic relationship among these three measures.

      2) What harmonic pattern are these measures based on? Consider both chord roots and actual positions and voice leading (as indicated by the figured bass) to answer this question.

      3) What degrees are tonicized in these measures (consider that Dm is the main key in this passage).

Example 17.3   W. A. Mozart, Symphony no. 41 in CM, *Jupiter,* K. 551, II, mm. 58–61

EXERCISE 17.5 Harmonize the following melody with a bass and RNs. The melody includes an extended tonicization (a secondary key area). What degree is tonicized? Make sure you take this secondary key area into account in both your harmonization and the RN analysis.

Gm:

(France)

EXERCISE 17.6 Realize the following sequential patterns involving consecutive secondary dominants. Be careful with the voice leading and the irregular resolution of the leading tone and the seventh. Provide RNs for progression a.

a.

b.

B♭M: I   V₇/vi   V₇/ii   V₇/V   V₇   V₇/IV   IV   V   I

KEYBOARD PROGRESSIONS   Play the following keyboard progressions in CM, GM, FM, DM, B♭M; and Cm, Em, Dm, Bm, and Gm, where minor mode applies. Listen to the secondary dominants and to the chromatic voice leading as you play.

♪ Example 17.5

Chapter 18

Secondary Leading-Tone Chords

EXERCISE 18.1   Analysis.

1. Identify with RNs (Roman numerals) all the tonicizations and secondary functions in the following examples.
   a) Example 18.1.

      Using your own music paper, realize a bass reduction for the Verdi passage. Use example 16.13 in the textbook as a reference for your reduction, in which you will show several levels of harmonic activity. In the first level (the "surface" level), show the role of tonic, dominant, and predominant chords using appropriate symbols. If any of these chords is prolonged or embellished by any other chord (such as secondary dominants), show it accordingly. In the following levels, first delete the prolongational chords, leaving only the basic harmonic structure at the phrase level, and finally the basic structure at the period level.
   b) Example 18.2.
   c) Refer back to example 16.1 (Bach, Chorale 107). Identify two tonicizations in the second phrase (mm. 17–18) that use secondary diminished seventh chords. Provide exact RNs.

2. a) Provide a RN analysis of example 18.3. Write the RNs in the spaces included under the chords.
   b) Identify on the score all the circled NCTs (nonchord tones). Provide labels (such as 4–3, 9–8, etc.) for suspensions where needed.

Example 18.1   G. Verdi, *Il trovatore,* Act II, no. 15, mm. 13–17.

Example 18.2   Fritz Kreisler, *Liebesfreud,* mm. 1–8.

♪♪ Example 18.3   Antonio Caldara, "Come raggio di sol," mm. 1–27

Example 18.3   Continued

EXERCISE 18.2   Write and resolve the following secondary diminished seventh chords. The resolution should be to the appropriate tonicized chord, in root position or inversion as required by the voice leading in the bass.

DM: vii°$_7$/V ____   EM: vii°$_5^6$ /ii ____   C♯m: vii°$_2^4$/ VI ____   GM: vii°$_7$/iii ____

Bm: vii°$_3^4$/ iv ____   Fm: vii°$_5^6$ /III ____   B♭M: vii°$_2^4$/ IV ____   F♯m: vii°$_3^4$/ III ____

Gm: vii°$_5^6$ / iv ____   FM: vii°$_7$/IV ____   Em: vii°$_2^4$/ V ____   D♭M: vii°$_3^4$/ vi ____

EXERCISE 18.3   Realize the following short progressions in four voices.

GM: I   vii°$^4_3$/V   V$_6$ I   FM: I   ii$^6_5$ vii°$_7$/V   V   I   EM: I   vii°$^6_5$/ii   ii   V   I

EXERCISE 18.4   Realize the following figured bass in four voices. Provide a RN analysis.

EXERCISE 18.5

1. Write progressions (bass and RNs) using the chords required in each case. Make sure you resolve the required chords correctly.

   a) vii°$^4_3$/V, vii°$^6_5$/iv, vii°$_7$/V.

   b) vii°$_7$/ii, vii°$^6_5$/vi, vii°$^6_5$/V.

a.

   F♯m:

b.

   B♭M:

2. Choose one of your own progressions from above, and use it as a harmonic basis to compose a phrase for a melodic instrument and keyboard accompaniment.

EXERCISE 18.6

1. Harmonize the following melody with a bass and RNs. If possible, follow the suggested harmonic rhythm. Harmonize the notes marked with an asterisk with a secondary diminished seventh chord. Include a secondary key area of III where required by the melody.

2. Once you are sure that your harmonization is correct, copy the melody again on your own music paper and, below it, provide a left-hand keyboard realization of your harmonization.

KEYBOARD PROGRESSIONS   Practice the following keyboard progressions in a variety of keys. (Suggested keys: CM, DM, AM, E♭M, A♭M, and their relative minors.)

Example 18.4

Chapter 19

Modulation to Closely Related Keys

EXERCISE 19.1 *Analysis.* Study and analyze the following modulations, and follow the steps listed below for each of them.

1. Identify (and write in the space below) the keys involved in the modulation.

2. Identify (and write in the space below) the modulation procedure from among the following:
    a) Diatonic pivot chord.
    b) Chromatic pivot chord.
    c) Chromatic modulation.
    d) Phrase modulation.
    e) Abrupt modulation.
    f) Sequential modulation or tonicizations.

3. If it is a pivot chord modulation, identify the exact pivot or pivots, and label it or them on the score with the pivot chord bracket notation, indicating the function of the chord in both keys.

4. For a chromatic modulation, circle the exact passage where chromatic voice leading is used to modulate.

5. For phrase, abrupt, or sequential modulations, mark the exact spot or spots where modulation occurs.

Examples for Analysis

1. Anthology, no. 12, Bach, French Suite no. 5, Gavotte, mm. 1–8.

2. Example 19.1.

♩♪ Example 19.1   A. Beach, "Elle et moi," mm. 13–23

à la vive é - tin - cel - - - - - -

le,

Le tro - ë - ne des champs a - vec

3. Anthology, no. 12, Bach, French Suite no. 5, Gavotte, mm. 9–16.

4. Example 19.2.

Example 19.2   W. A. Mozart, Piano Sonata in CM, K. 330, II, mm. 21–28

5. Example 19.3.

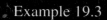
Example 19.3   R. Schumann, "Nachtlied," op. 96, no. 1, mm. 7–14

Ruh,   in al - len   Wip - feln   spü - rest du   kaum ei - nen Hauch.

6. Example 19.4.

Example 19.4   R. Schumann, "Der Dichter spricht," from *Scenes from Childhood,* op.15, mm. 1–8

7. Example 19.5.

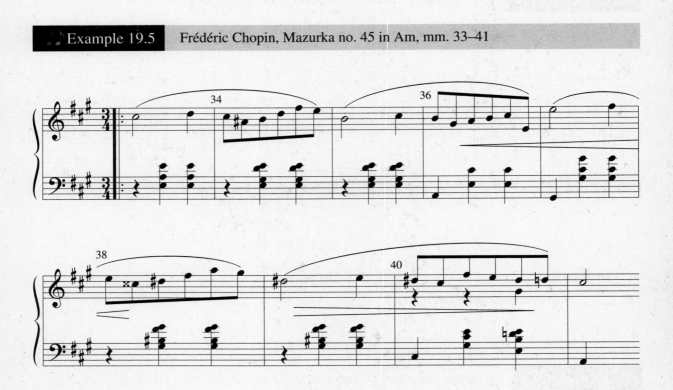

Example 19.5   Frédéric Chopin, Mazurka no. 45 in Am, mm. 33–41

8. Example 19.6.

Example 19.6   Maria Szymanowska, Etude in Dm, mm. 1–9

EXERCISE 19.2   The following statements refer to diatonic pivot chord relationships. Fill in the blank in each statement.

1. ii in _____ becomes iv in Am.

2. _____ in AM becomes vi in DM.

3. vi in FM becomes ii in _____.

4. ii° in Bm becomes _____ in DM.

EXERCISE 19.3   The following two progressions represent modulations by diatonic pivot chord.

Progression a. Provide RNs (Roman numerals) for the given bass, accounting for the modulation and indicating the pivot chord with the usual bracket. Use secondary dominants or diminished seventh chords where possible.

a.

Progression b. Write a bass line for the given RNs. Be careful to modulate to the right key.

b.

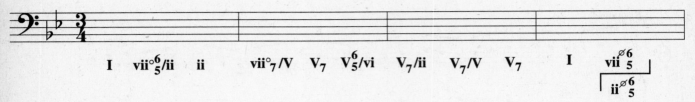

$$I \quad vii°^6_5/ii \quad ii \quad vii°_7/V \quad V_7 \quad V^6_5/vi \quad V_7/ii \quad V_7/V \quad V_7 \quad\quad I \quad vii^{ø6}_5$$

$$ii^{ø6}_5$$

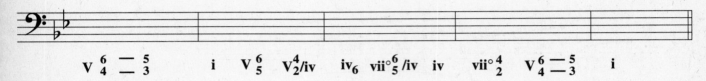

$$V \, ^6_4 - \, ^5_3 \quad\quad i \quad V^6_5 \quad V^4_2/iv \quad iv_6 \quad vii°^6_5/iv \quad iv \quad vii°^4_2 \quad V^6_4 - ^5_3 \quad i$$

EXERCISE 19.4 The following progression represents a chromatic modulation. Write a bass line for the given RNs.

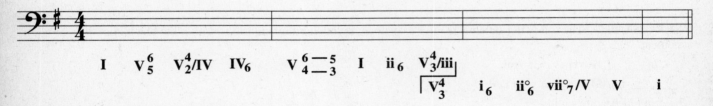

$$I \quad V^6_5 \quad V^4_2/IV \quad IV_6 \quad\quad V\,^6_4 - ^5_3 \quad I \quad ii_6 \quad V^4_3/iii$$

$$V^4_3 \quad i_6 \quad ii°_6 \quad vii°_7/V \quad V \quad i$$

EXERCISE 19.5 Realize the following progression in four voices.

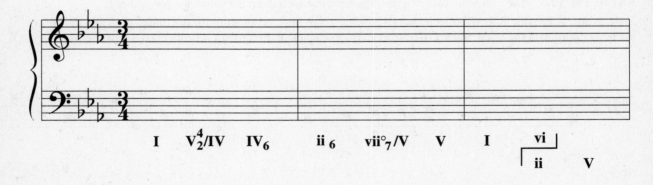

$$I \quad V^4_2/IV \quad IV_6 \quad\quad ii_6 \quad vii°_7/V \quad V \quad I \quad\quad vi$$

$$ii \quad V$$

$$I \quad vii°_7/IV \quad IV \quad vii°_7/V \quad V\,^6_4 - ^5_3 \quad I$$

EXERCISE 19.6 After you are sure that your bass line for exercise 19.4 is correct, realize the progression in four voices in the space below.

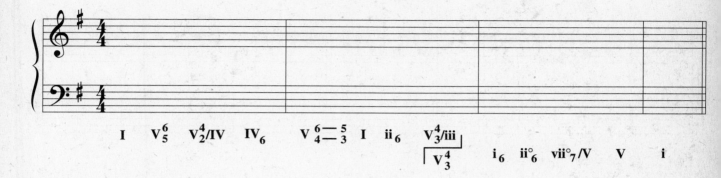

$$\text{I} \quad \text{V}^6_5 \quad \text{V}^4_2/\text{IV} \quad \text{IV}_6 \quad \text{V}^{6-5}_{4-3} \quad \text{I} \quad \text{ii}_6 \quad \text{V}^4_3/\text{iii}$$

$$\text{V}^4_3 \quad \text{i}_6 \quad \text{ii}°_6 \quad \text{vii}°_7/\text{V} \quad \text{V} \quad \text{i}$$

EXERCISE 19.7 Write the following modulations (bass and RNs). Choose an appropriate pivot chord for each of them, and indicate it with the customary bracket.

1. A modulation from Fm to A♭M. Use the following chords somewhere in your progression, along with any other chords you wish: vii°$^4_3$/V, vii°$^6_5$/ii, and an irregular resolution of V$^6_5$/V.

2. A modulation from DM to GM. Use the following chords somewhere in your progression: V$^4_3$/vi, vii°$^4_2$/V, and vii°$^4_3$/IV.

3. A chromatic modulation from EM to F♯m, using secondary chords in various inversions in the process of establishing both keys.

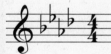

EXERCISE 19.8 Harmonize the following chorale ("Jesu, meine Freude") with a bass line and RNs, accounting for possible modulations. After you are sure that your harmonization works, add the two inner voices.

EXERCISE 19.9 Write simple keyboard accompaniments for the following modulating periods by Haydn. Provide RNs for your harmonizations, and indicate your pivot chord in each case.

KEYBOARD PROGRESSIONS   Practice the keyboard progressions from example 19.7 in a variety of keys. Hear and understand the modulating process in each case (by either pivot chord or chromatic motion).

Example 19.7

Chapter 20

Small Forms: Binary and Ternary

EXERCISE 20.1 *Analysis.* Analyze the following pieces. For each of them, determine and discuss the formal and tonal types, the key areas in the complete piece, and construct a bubble diagram using the given line. The diagram should show sections (labeled with letters) and tonal motion. As an additional exercise, provide bass reductions for some or all of the pieces, showing the tonal type, the long-range tonal motion, and the key areas. Use the various diagrams and reductions in this chapter as models.

1. Anthology, no. 12, Bach, French Suite no. 5, Gavotte.

   a) Form and formal type:

   b) Key areas:

   c) Bubble diagram and bass reduction:

2. Anthology, no. 7, *Notebook for Anna Magdalena Bach,* Polonaise.

   a) Form and formal type:

   b) Key areas:

   c) Bubble diagram and bass reduction:

3. Example 20.1.

   a) Form and formal type:

   b) Key areas:

   c) Bubble diagram and bass reduction:

♪♪ Example 20.1   L. v. Beethoven, String Quartet in B♭M, op. 18, no. 6, Trio

4. Anthology, no. 37, Kuhlau, Sonatina, II.
   a) Form and formal type:

   b) Key areas:

   c) Bubble diagram and bass reduction:

---

5. Example 20.2.
   a) Form and formal type:

   b) Key areas:

   c) Bubble diagram and bass reduction:

♪♪ Example 20.2   J. S. Bach, Bourrée

6. Anthology, no. 44, Chopin, Mazurka no. 43 in Gm.

   a) Form and formal type:

   b) Key areas:

   c) Bubble diagram and bass reduction:

EXERCISE 20.2 *Analytical paper.* Choose one of the pieces you just studied in exercise 20.1, and write a brief analytical paper on it. With good narrative prose, discuss form, formal and tonal types, sections, key areas and tonal motion, and thematic/motivic relationships. Identify also special compositional techniques (such as imitation, sequence, textural inversion between hands, etc.), and discuss the techniques of motivic and thematic development used in the piece. Attach (and comment on) a bass reduction and a bubble diagram. You may use the various analytical discussions of pieces you have found in this chapter's text as possible models for your paper (and your narrative).

EXERCISE 20.3   Harmonize the following chorale ("Von Gott will ich nicht lassen") with a bass line and RNs (Roman numerals), accounting for possible modulations. As an additional exercise, you can also fill in inner voices.

EXERCISE 20.4   Write two different harmonizations for the following chorale tune ("O Haupt voll Blut und Wunden"). Bass and RNs are sufficient, but as an additional exercise you can also fill in inner voices.

EXERCISE 20.5   Write a keyboard accompaniment for the following melody, and provide RNs for your harmonization. What formal and tonal types does this melody represent?

EXERCISE 20.6   Compose a brief binary piece for piano on the basis of the given opening motive.

1. First, write a modulating period, modulating to V (you may want to do exercise 20.5 from worksheet 20 first).

2. Then, write a short developmental phrase using the initial motive, perhaps sequentially, and leading to V. This in turn will lead to a return of the tonic.

3. Write again the original phrase (the return), only now it should not modulate, but it should instead remain in the tonic key.

4. Use some of the many binary pieces we have studied in this chapter as models. The binary melody you just harmonized in exercise 20.5 is also a good and simple model. You may wish to write the melody first and then the left hand (as in exercise 20.5), or do both tasks at the same time.

Chapter 21

Contrapuntal Genres

EXERCISE 21.1   Analyze Bach's chorale prelude on the chorale "Wenn wir in höchsten Nöten sein," BWV 641. You will find this prelude in the *Orgelbüchlein,* and also in the Burkhart anthology. The original chorale tune is provided in example 21.1.

1. Where and how does the chorale tune appear in this prelude? Circle all the pitches of the original chorale melody in Bach's version.

2. How would you describe the texture of this piece?

Example 21.1   Chorale melody "Wenn wir in höchsten Nöten sein"

3. How are the accompanying voices related with the chorale tune?

4. Is there any motivic cohesion in the accompanying voices? Where does the motive come from?

5. Circle, on the score, all the appearances of the unifying motive. Does it always appear in the same form? For instance, in mm. 1–2, there are four instances of the motive. How are they related?

6. Mark, on the score, all the cadences and what degrees they are on. Is there any modulation? To what key?

EXERCISE 21.2   Write a brief analytical paper on Bach's Invention no. 4 in Dm (score and recording available at the library). You may use the discussion of Invention no. 3 in DM in chapter 21 of the textbook as a model. The organization by sections used in that analysis is perfectly appropriate for your paper. Make sure you discuss the following aspects of the Dm invention:

1. Sections and their function (exposition, episodes, return, codetta). Cadences and key areas. Any pedals? What is their harmonic and formal function?
2. How are all the keys in the piece related among themselves?
3. Thematic content: What are the musical characteristics of the subject? Is the subject always present? Does it appear in any varied forms (such as inverted, or elaborated in any way)?
4. What developmental techniques are used and where (circle of fifths, sequence, fragmentation, etc.)? What is the role of imitation in the piece? Are there sections of "give-and-take" texture?

EXERCISE 21.3   Analyze Mozart's String Quartet, K. 173, IV (Fugue). Answer the following questions, and turn in an annotated copy of the score (which you will find at your music library).

1. Exposition:
   a) How long is the subject?

b) Is the answer real or tonal?

c) Is there a countersubject? If yes, where?

d) Is there a bridge? Where?

e) What are its specific formal and tonal functions?

f) The exposition ends with the first full authentic cadence in the piece. Where, and in what key?

2. Middle sections:
   a) Episode 1 (mm. numbers):   Its tonal function is:
   b) Middle entry group 1: It begins in m.   in the key of
                              It ends in m.   in the key of
   c) Episode 2 (mm. numbers):   Its tonal function is:
   d) The entry in m. 28 is in the key of:
   e) Episode 3 (mm. 31–35) leads to a series of entries in mm. 35–44. Mark all of them on the score. What happened to the subject in these entries?

   What is the effect of whatever happened to the subject from a metric point of view?
   What name does this type of section have in a fugue?

   f) Mark on the score the entries in mm. 45–51. What is the key?
   g) Measures 52–61: Mark the entries. Again, what happens to the subject? What kind of section is this?

Measures 58–61: What kind of texture is this?

Why? Where does it lead?

What is the chord in m. 61?

Why does it have a fermata?

3. Closing sections:
   a) What is the key of mm. 62-end?
   b) What is the formal/tonal function of the section beginning in m. 62?

   c) Considering the metric relationship among entries in this section (mm. 62–69), what is this section?

   d) How are the viola and second violin subjects related to the cello and first violin in these measures?

   e) Measures 70–73: What is this section? How are the entries related (metrically) to those in the previous section?

   f) Is there a pedal in the closing section? If yes, on what scale degree?

EXERCISE 21.4   On your own music paper, write four fugal subjects, in different meters and keys. Determine whether the answer to each of your subjects should be real or tonal. Then, write the appropriate answer for each of them.

Chapter 22

Modal Mixture; Variation Forms

EXERCISE 22.1 Analysis.

1. Analyze and explain the type of modal mixture in the following examples. If borrowed chords are involved, be specific as to what they are.

   a) Example 22.1.

   b) Example 22.2.

   c) Anthology, no. 54, Verdi, *Il trovatore,* Act II, no. 14, mm. 21–24. Compare also the beginning and ending keys.

Example 22.1   Haydn, String Quartet in B♭M, op. 64, no. 3, I, mm. 33–39

Example 22.2   Brahms, Piano Quartet, op. 60, III, mm. 1–2

d) Example 22.3.

Example 22.3   J. S. Bach, "Vor deinem Tron tret' ich hiermit," BWV 668, mm. 44–45

e) Example 22.4.

Example 22.4   Joseph Haydn, String Quartet in GM, op. 9, no. 3, I, mm. 20–24

f) Anthology, no. 47, Schumann, "Ich grolle nicht," mm. 1–4.

g) Example 22.5.

Example 22.5   J. Haydn, String Quartet in DM, op. 64, no. 5, III, mm. 9–17

EXERCISE 22.3   Harmonize the following melody with a left-hand keyboard figuration, using borrowed chords where possible. Be sure to check your outer-voice frame for correct voice leading.

FM:

EXERCISE 22.4   Write a nonmodulating period using the given motive, and provide a keyboard harmonization. Use several instances of mixture (borrowed chords, change of mode) in your harmonization.

KEYBOARD PROGRESSIONS   Practice the keyboard progressions from example 22.6 in a variety of keys. Because these progressions use chords from the minor mode borrowed in the major mode, they should be played *only in major keys*.

Example 22.6

Chapter 23

The Neapolitan and Augmented Sixth Chords

EXERCISE 23.1   *Analysis.* For each of the following examples, identify possible Neapolitan or +6 chords.

1. For ♭II chords, verify and mark the voice leading of the voice with ♭2̂. Is the ♭II chord in first inversion or root position?

2. For +6 chords, identify the type ("nationality"). If it is Gr +6, is it spelled with a ♭3̂ or a ♯2̂?

3. In all cases, provide RNs (Roman numerals) for the actual ♭II or +6 chord, and also for the chords that precede and follow it.

4. What chord precedes the ♭II or +6 chord? Is the ♭II chord tonicized?

5. Does the ♭II or +6 chord resolve directly to V? Does it resolve to V through some other harmonies? Are parallel 5ths avoided?

Examples for Analysis

1. Example 23.1.

2. Anthology, no. 38, *Erlkönig,* mm. 113–123.

Example 23.1   W. A. Mozart, Piano Concerto in AM, K. 488, II, mm. 1–12

3. Anthology, no. 35, Beethoven, *Waldstein* Sonata, mm. 235–239.

4. Example 23.2.

Example 23.2   F. Chopin, Mazurka op. 7, no. 2, mm. 11–16

5. Example 23.3.

Example 23.3   W. A. Mozart, Symphony no. 39 in E♭M, K. 543, IV, mm. 130–137

6. Example 23.4.

7. Example 23.5.

Example 23.4   Haydn, String Quartet in DM, op. 64, no. 5, I, mm. 46–50

Example 23.5   Gioachino Rossini, *Petite messe solennelle,* Credo, mm. 14–18

8. Example 23.6a.

Example 23.6b.

Example 23.6   L. v. Beethoven, String Quartet in Cm, op. 18, no.4, IV, mm. 5–8 and 147–153

EXERCISE 23.3   Realize the following progression in four voices. Provide a RN analysis.

EXERCISE 23.4   Harmonize the following melody by Schubert ("Der Müller und der Bach") with a bass and RNs. Use ♭II₆ chords where possible. One of the ♭II₆ chords should be resolved to V through a vii°₇/V. The melody also allows, in mm. 9–12, for a circle-of-fifths segment and for some tonicizations. Explore these possibilities in your harmonization. As an additional exercise, write a version of your harmonization for voice and piano on your own music paper.

Where a true heart pines away for love, there droop the lilies on every bank.
Clouds conceal the moon so that men may not see her tears. Angels close
their eyes, and cry and sing the soul to rest.

After you write the harmonization, write brief statements on the following questions.

1. Are the $\flat II_6$ chords used for expressive purposes in this song? What are the words and/or concepts the $\flat II_6$ chords harmonize?

2. What formal/tonal type, of the ones we studied in chapter 20, defines the passage you harmonized? Name the type, and explain your reasons for choosing it. To answer this question, consider carefully the sections and tonal motion in this song. Notice that the passage does not feature any inner repeat signs. If it did (and it certainly could), where would they be (think of the formal and tonal function of each section)?

KEYBOARD PROGRESSIONS   Practice the keyboard progressions from example 23.9 in a variety of M and m keys. Hear the sound and resolution of the ♭II₆ or +6 chords in the progressions. Notice especially (and enjoy!) the interesting harmonization of the descending chromatic bass, which you can now realize with chords you have studied (example 23.9d).

♪ Example 23.9

Chapter 24

Chromatic Modulatory Techniques: Modulation to Distantly Related Keys

EXERCISE 24.1   Analysis.

1. The following modulation features a chromatic pivot chord. Analyze the complete passage with RNs (Roman numerals), and explain the modulation and the pivot chord.

♪♪ Example 24.1   L. v. Beethoven, Six Variations, op. 76, Var. VI, mm. 27–38

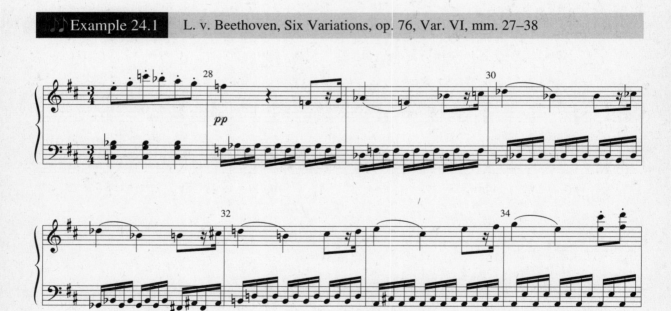

2. The following examples feature the ♭II key area and/or modulations by enharmonic reinterpretation of +6. Analyze each of them, identify the modulations or the ♭II key area, the keys involved, and the exact function of the pivot chord in each of the keys.

   a) Example 24.2.

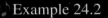 Example 24.2   F. Schubert, Piano Sonata in Am, op. 164, I, mm. 57–67

b) Anthology, no. 51, Liszt, *Consolation*, no. 4. The phrase in mm. 16–18 is in DM. A sudden phrase modulation takes place in m. 18. To what key? How does the chord in m. 18, beats 1–2, function in each of the
keys?

c) Example 24.3.

  1) The main key of the passage is FM. What secondary key area of FM is featured?

  2) Explain the return to FM in mm. 47–53.

♪ Example 24.3   F. Schubert, Piano Sonata in Am, op. 164, I, mm. 41–53

3. The passage by Schubert in example 24.4 begins in B♭m.

   a) What is the chord in mm. 139–140, and to what chord does it resolve?

   b) What is the key area in mm. 152–159?

   c) The modulation to this second key area takes place in mm. 146–152. Explain how this modulation works.

   d) What is the key in mm. 162–167?

   e) What is the chord in mm. 160–161, and how does it function in AM? Have we seen this same sonority elsewhere in this passage in a different key and with a different function?

   f) The modulation in mm. 157–162 is to a closely related key by means of a diatonic pivot chord. Explain.

   g) Comment on the compositional/contrapuntal techniques used in this passage, especially in mm. 142–166.

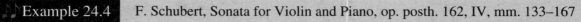

Example 24.4   F. Schubert, Sonata for Violin and Piano, op. posth. 162, IV, mm. 133–167

4. The following examples feature modulation by enharmonic reinterpretation of vii°₇ chords. Analyze each of them, identify the modulations, the keys involved, and the exact function of the pivot chord in each of the keys.

a) Example 24.5.

Example 24.5   L. v. Beethoven, Piano Sonata in Cm, op. 13, *Pathétique,* I, mm. 133–136

b) Example 24.6. This passage begins in AM.

1) What key area is featured in mm. 141–144?

2) What is the function of the first chord in m. 140 in each of the keys?

3) The same chord is featured again in m. 145, leading back to AM. What is its function here?

♪ Example 24.6   L. v. Beethoven, Piano Sonata in AM, op. 2 no. 2, IV, mm. 138–148

5. After you go over the "Further Analysis" section of this chapter, analyze the following examples of chromatic linear modulation processes, and identify in them *fonte* or *monte* patterns.

   a) Example 24.7.

Example 24.7   Antonio Soler, Sonata, no. 86, in DM, mm. 13–26

b) Example 24.8.

Example 24.8   Jean Philippe Rameau, *Les Indes Galantes,* Gavotte

EXERCISE 24.2   Write the following chromatic pivot chord modulations (bass and RNs, with indication of the pivot chord).

1. From FM to AM using $\flat$II$_6$ of AM as a pivot.

FM:

2. From AM to BM using a secondary dominant in AM as pivot.

AM:

3. From B$\flat$M to CM using a vii°$_7$ chord with a secondary function in both keys.

B$\flat$M:

EXERCISE 24.3   The following RNs represent modulations by enharmonic reinterpretation of the Gr +6 chord. Write the bass line for each progression, and indicate what key we have modulated to in each case.

a.

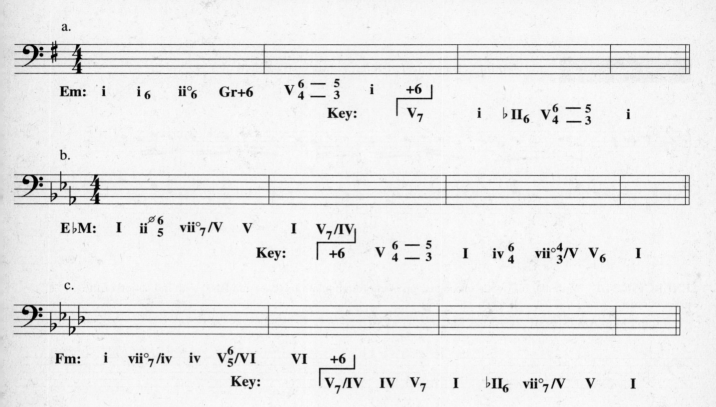

Em: i   i$_6$ ii°$_6$ Gr+6   V$^6_4$ — $^5_3$ i   +6⌐

Key: V$_7$ i   ♭II$_6$ V$^6_4$ — $^5_3$ i

b.

E♭M: I   ii$^{ø6}_5$ vii°$_7$/V   V   I   V$_7$/IV⌐

Key: ⌐+6   V$^6_4$ — $^5_3$ I   iv$^6_4$ vii°$^4_3$/V   V$_6$ I

c.

Fm: i   vii°$_7$/iv   iv   V$^6_5$/VI   VI   +6⌐

Key: ⌐V$_7$/IV   IV   V$_7$ I   ♭II$_6$ vii°$_7$/V   V   I

EXERCISE 24.4   Write the following modulating progression in four voices. Provide both enharmonic spellings for the pivot chord. Write the key signature for the new key after the double bar (in the space marked with an asterisk).

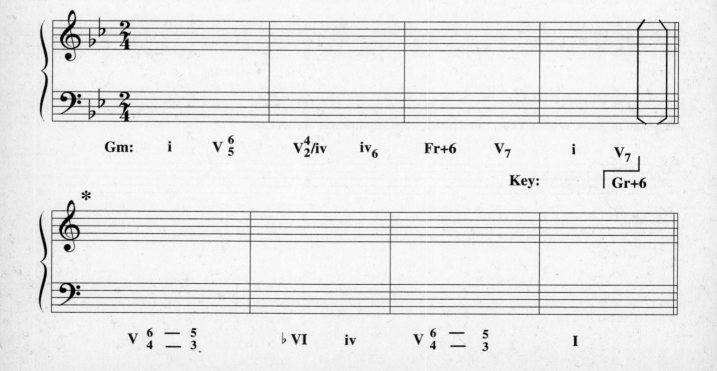

Gm: i   V$^6_5$ V$^4_2$/iv   iv$_6$ Fr+6   V$_7$ i   V$_7$⌐

Key: ⌐Gr+6

*

V$^6_4$ — $^5_3$ ♭VI   iv   V$^6_4$ — $^5_3$ I

EXERCISE 24.5

1. Write and resolve vii°₇ in E♭M in exercise 24.5a. This chord may be used to modulate to three other major keys by respelling it enharmonically. Indicate the keys, and provide the spelling (leaving the chord in the same position), the correct RN, and the correct resolution to the corresponding tonic in each of the new keys. For a reference of what you are doing exactly, see example 24.16b in the textbook (although in that example the chords are not resolved).

2. In exercise 24.5b follow the same process as in 24.5a, but now show how vii°₇ in Gm functions in three other minor keys.

a.   b.

key 1: E♭M   key 2:   key 3:   key 4:   key 1: Gm   key 2:   key 3:   key 4:

3. The following statements refer to enharmonically respelled vii°₇ chords. Fill in the blank in each statement.

    a) vii°₇ in A♭ becomes _____ in D.

    b) _____ in E becomes vii°⁴₂ in B♭.

    c) vii°⁴₃ in _____ becomes vii°₇ in A.

    d) vii°⁴₂ in F becomes vii°₇ in _____.

EXERCISE 24.6   The following RNs represent a modulation by enharmonic reinterpretation of vii°₇. Write the bass line, and indicate what key we have modulated to.

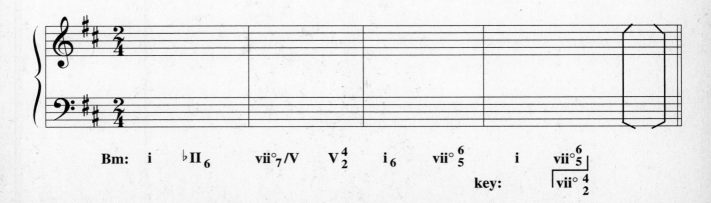

AM: I   vii°₇/vi   vi   vii°⁴₃/ii   ii₆   V   I   vii°₇/ii

key: ⌐ vii°⁴₃   I₆   ii₇   V⁶₄——⁵₃   I

EXERCISE 24.7   Write the following modulating progression in four voices. Provide both enharmonic spellings for the pivot chord. Write the key signature for the new key after the double bar (in the space marked with an asterisk).

Bm: i   ♭II₆   vii°₇/V   V⁴₂   i₆   vii°⁶₅   i   vii°⁶₅

key: ⌐ vii°⁴₂

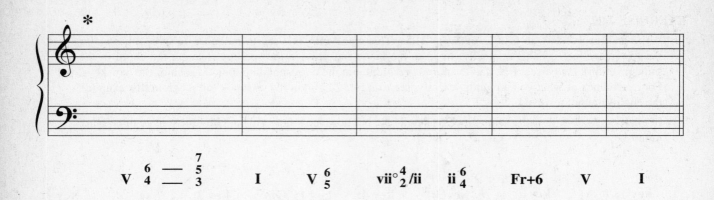

$$V \; ^6_4 \; — \; ^7_5_3 \qquad I \qquad V \; ^6_5 \qquad vii°\;^4_2/ii \qquad ii \; ^6_4 \qquad Fr+6 \qquad V \qquad I$$

EXERCISE 24.8   Write your own modulating progressions (bass and RNs) using Gr +6 and vii°$_7$ chords as pivots.

1. A modulation from Fm to Em using an enharmonic reinterpretation of the Gr +6.

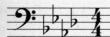

Fm:

2. A modulation from AM to Cm using an enharmonic reinterpretation of vii°$^6_5$ in AM.

AM:

KEYBOARD PROGRESSIONS   Practice the keyboard progressions from example 24.9 in a variety of keys. Hear and understand the modulating process in each case (by either chromatic pivot chord or enharmonic reinterpretation). If you are sufficiently proficient at the keyboard, practice improvising some similar progressions, especially using +6 and vii°$_7$ chords to modulate to distant keys.

Example 24.9

Chapter 25

Modulation to Distantly Related Keys II; Linear Chromaticism I

EXERCISE 25.1   Analysis.

1. Study the chordal relationships in the following passage, and explain with the correct terms how the chords are related.

♪♪ Example 25.1   G. Verdi, *Otello*, Act I, Scene III, mm. 46–50

2. Study the following modulations. For each of them, determine the following points:
   a) What keys are involved?
   b) How are the keys related (diatonic third, chromatic third, half step, etc.)
   c) What is the RN relationship between the keys? (Be aware of possible enharmonic spellings of keys.)
   d) What type of modulation is it?
   e) If it is a common tone (CT) modulation, what is the CT? Or is there, perhaps, more than one CT?

f) What are the functions of the triads used in the CT modulation?

Examples for Analysis

1. Example 25.2.

Example 25.2   L. v. Beethoven, Trio in Cm, op. 1, no. 3, IV, mm. 167–173

2. Example 25.3.

  a. First, study the modulation in mm. 9–12.

  b. Then analyze the return to the original key in mm. 12–16.

Example 25.3   F. Schubert, Waltz in A♭M, op. 9 no. 2

3. The following passages include examples of altered triads, Fr +6 as an altered dominant, embellishing +6, or CT°7 chords. Identify and label the particular chord illustrated in each example, and determine its exact linear function (passing, neighbor/embellishing, etc.).

a) Example 25.4.

Example 25.4   R. Schumann, "Ich kann's nicht fassen," from *Frauenliebe und Leben,* mm. 17–23

b) Example 25.5.

Example 25.5   J. Brahms, Symphony no. 4 in Em, op. 98, IV, mm. 1–8

c) Example 25.6.

  1) Several of this chapter's chords are present in this fragment. One of them actually appears in three different keys. Another one is featured at the cadence. Identify and label all of them.

  2) What are the three keys featured in this example? How are they related?

Example 25.6   Jean Sibelius, *Finlandia*, op. 26, mm. 1–23

d) Example 25.7.

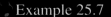 Example 25.7   F. Schubert, "Moment Musical," op. 94, no. 6, mm. 29–36

EXERCISE 25.2

1. List the six triads (or keys) related by chromatic third to each of the following triads (or keys). Write down both the triad name and the RN that indicates its relationship with the original triad.

2. Then, circle the four triads that have a CT with the original triad.

FM:

BM:

Gm:

C#m:

EXERCISE 25.3   Write a CT modulation in four voices, from Fm to a key of your choice, related with Fm by chromatic third. Include a secondary dominant and a Fr +6 in the first key area (Fm), and a tonicized ♭II chord in the second key area.

Fm:

EXERCISE 25.4   Realize the following short progressions in four voices. Pay attention to the RN quality (uppercase or lowercase), which may denote a chromatic third relationship (for instance, I–III is not the same, of course, as I–iii).

a.   b.

FM: I   VI   V⁺   I   Bm: i   Gr+6   V⁺   i

c.   d.

F♯m: i   V⁺   V⁺⁴₂   i₆   ii°̸₇   V°⁴₃   i   EM: I   ♭III   V°⁴₃   I

BbM: I   emb+6   I   III   I   AM: I   bII₆   vii°₇/V   V⁺   I   CT°7   I

EXERCISE 25.5   Write a common-tone modulation from EbM to bVI, in four voices. Spell the bVI key enharmonically. Include an embellishing +6 and a bII₆ in the EbM area, and a CT°7 and a cadential V°⁴₃ in the bVI area.

EbM:

KEYBOARD PROGRESSIONS   Practice the keyboard progressions in example 25.8 in a variety of keys. Hear and understand the CT modulations to chromatic third–related keys. And pay attention to the voice leading for the linear chromatic chords included in these progressions.

Example 25.8

Chapter 26

Introduction to Large Forms

EXERCISE 26.1   Write a short analytical paper on Brahms's Sonata no. 2 for Violin and Piano, op. 100, I, in sonata form. The score and a recording will be available at your music library. The score can also be found in the Arlin anthology *(Music Sources)*. You can use the analysis of Mozart's CM sonata in chapter 26 of the textbook, as well as the guided analysis of Beethoven's *Waldstein* sonata in the same chapter, as models for the organization of your paper. Turn in an annotated copy of the score.

The following are some specific questions about this particular movement by Brahms which you should address in your paper.

1. How is the P area structured? Is there a single P theme?

2. How many different S themes are there? Is there a C theme?

3. What marks the end of the exposition and the beginning of the development?

4. What are the themes on which Brahms bases the development?

5. Comment on the use of (at least) the following techniques in the development: hemiola, canonic imitation, thematic inversion, diminution, fragmentation, and pedal.

6. Is there a retransition? Is it on the customary V harmony?

7. Compare carefully the recapitulation and the exposition, and comment on what is the same and what is different.

8. The movement features a coda which functions as a second development. Explain where it begins and ends, and its thematic and tonal contents.

9. While in the exposition the P theme is stated first by the piano, and then by the violin, the equivalent statement of P in the recapitulation combines the instruments in a different way (how?). Does the statement of the beginning of P by the violin (which is missing at the beginning of the recapitulation) come later in the movement?

10. Provide a complete analysis of key areas and tonal motion in the movement, as well as some kind of formal diagram and/or long-range bass reduction.

EXERCISE 26.2   Analyze Beethoven's String Quartet in Cm, op. 18 n. 4, IV, in rondo form. The score and the recording will be available at your music library. The score can also be found in the Arlin anthology *(Music Sources)*. Turn in an annotated copy of the score with indications of thematic/sectional content and key areas for the complete movement.

Provide some kind of formal diagram and/or long-range bass reduction for the complete movement, and answer the following questions:

1. What type of rondo form is this?

2. What is the formal design of the refrain?

3. The cadences in mm. 8, 12, and 16 are all approached by means of the same type of chord. What is it?

4. What is the formal design of the first episode?

5. How are the keys of the refrain and first episode related?

6. Compare the textures of the refrain and the first episode. How are they contrasting? What contrapuntal techniques can you identify in the first episode?

7. How is the first return of the refrain different from the original refrain?

8. What is the formal design of the second episode? How is this episode contrasting tonally?

9. How is second return of the refrain different from the previous statements of the same material?

10. What is the formal function of mm. 111–116?

11. What is the section that begins in m. 117? Have we heard this material before, and what is different here from what we heard before?

12. Explain the formal structure of mm. 125–136. What is the function of mm. 132–136 within this passage?

13. An apparent final return of the refrain begins in m. 137. What is the character, however, of the section that begins in that measure? What key areas are touched on?

14. What is the formal function of mm. 154–162? What section do they lead to? What is the distinguishing characteristic of this new presentation of old material?

15. What is the section that begins in m. 178?

16. Comment on motivic coherence in this movement.
    a) How are the motives in mm. 1 and 9 related?

    b) How are the two violin lines in mm. 9–12 related? Do the viola and cello in the same measures display a similar relationship?

    c) Is the theme of the first episode (motive in mm. 17–18 and 25–26) related to the opening motive in any way? And what about the thematic material of the second episode (m. 75)?

Chapter 27

Expanding Functional Tonality: Extended Tertian Chords; Linear Chromaticism II

EXERCISE 27.1   Analysis.

1. The following passages include examples of extended tertian chords. Identify and label these chords, and verify the resolution of the dissonant chord members.

   a) Example 27.1. Explain the resolution of the extended tertian chord in this example. What kind of a linear, embellishing chord does Beethoven use to connect the dominant and the tonic harmonies?

Example 27.1   L. v. Beethoven, Six Variations, op. 76, Variation V, mm. 5–8

b) Example 27.2.

Example 27.2   Pyotr Ilich Tchaikovsky, *The Sleeping Beauty,* Act I, no. 1, March, mm. 1–5

c) Example 27.3.

Example 27.3   Maurice Ravel, Sonatina, I, mm. 22–23

d) Example 27.4.

1) What are the two chords in m. 182?

2) Measure 183 contains a single harmony, an Em tonic chord. How do you explain the pitches in beat 1?

Example 27.4   William Grant Still, *Pastorela,* for Violin and Piano, mm. 180–192.

3) Think of mm. 188–192 as a modulation from Em to CM. What chord is used to modulate, and how does it function in each of the keys?

4) Provide the exact RN (Roman numeral) for the CM tonic chord in m. 192.

♪♩ Example 27.5   Richard Wagner, *Tristan und Isolde,* Prelude to Act III, mm. 30–43.

e) Example 27.5.

1) The basic harmonic content of this passage (in Fm) can be reduced to two chords. The first one is pro-
    longed in mm. 30–37, and the second one in mm. 38–43. What are the chords?

2) These two harmonies are repeatedly embellished by means of the same two types of linear chords,
    which you will first find in mm. 30–31. What are they?

2. The following examples include chromatic sequences. Name the exact type of sequence, and provide the necessary figures to identify the sequential pattern.

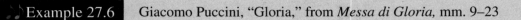

♪ Example 27.6   Giacomo Puccini, "Gloria," from *Messa di Gloria,* mm. 9–23

a) Example 27.6.

   1) Identify and analyze the chromatic sequence in this excerpt.

   2) Study the chord succession in mm. 15–17. How are these chords related (take into consideration root relationships and triadic quality)?

   3) Explain the modulation from CM to E♭M in mm. 18–20. What key relationship is this? What chord is used to modulate, and how does it function in each key?

b) Example 27.7. In this excerpt you will find two of the sequence types we have studied in this chapter.

3. Example 27.8.

   a) On a separate sheet, explain the linear process in mm. 17–25 using the same concepts we applied to the analysis of Chopin's Prelude no. 4 in Em. Provide a diagram for these measures similar to the graph in example 27.20a of the textbook.

   b) What degree is tonicized in mm. 29–30?

Example 27.7   Antonio Vivaldi, "Laudamus Te," from *Gloria,* op. 103, no. 3, mm. 92–109

Example 27.8   F. Chopin, Mazurka in Am, op. 7 no. 2, mm. 17–32.

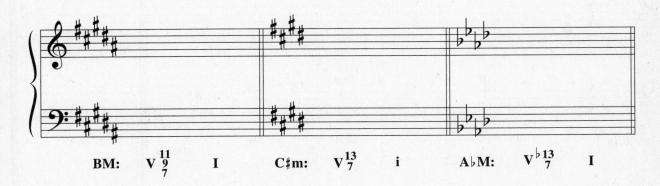

EXERCISE 27.2   Write and resolve the following extended tertian chords in four voices.

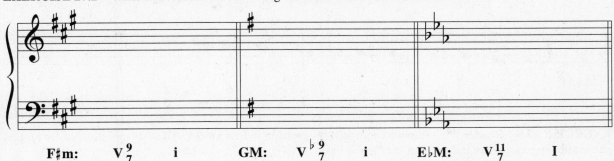

$$\text{F}\sharp\text{m:} \quad \text{V}^{9}_{7} \quad \text{i} \qquad \text{GM:} \quad \text{V}^{\flat 9}_{7} \quad \text{i} \qquad \text{E}\flat\text{M:} \quad \text{V}^{11}_{7} \quad \text{I}$$

$$\text{BM:} \quad \text{V}^{11}_{\substack{9\\7}} \quad \text{I} \qquad \text{C}\sharp\text{m:} \quad \text{V}^{13}_{7} \quad \text{i} \qquad \text{A}\flat\text{M:} \quad \text{V}^{\flat 13}_{7} \quad \text{I}$$

EXERCISE 27.3   Realize the following progression in four voices.

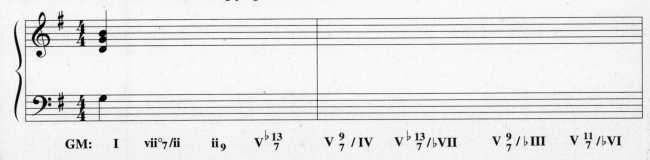

$$\text{GM:} \quad \text{I} \quad \text{vii}°_{7}/\text{ii} \quad \text{ii}_{9} \quad \text{V}^{\flat 13}_{7} \quad \text{V}^{9}_{7}/\text{IV} \quad \text{V}^{\flat 13}_{7}/\flat\text{VII} \quad \text{V}^{9}_{7}/\flat\text{III} \quad \text{V}^{11}_{7}/\flat\text{VI}$$

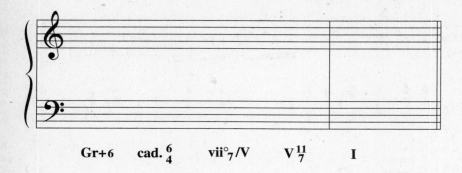

Gr+6   cad. $^6_4$ vii°$_7$/V   V$^{11}_7$ I

EXERCISE 27.4   Realize the following sequential progression in four voices. Although accidentals have not been indicated in the figured bass, all $^6_5$ chords should be inverted Mm$_7$ sonorities.

A♭M:

EXERCISE 27.5   Realize the following sequential progression in four voices. All necessary accidentals for this chromatic progression are indicated in the figured bass.

Gm:

EXERCISE 27.6   Write an omnibus progression prolonging V$_7$ in AM.

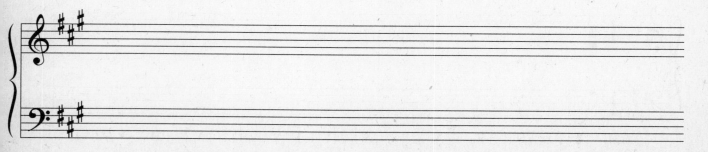

EXERCISE 27.7   On your own music paper, compose a phrase or a period for piano using a chromatic descending 5–6 sequence.

KEYBOARD PROGRESSIONS   Practice the following keyboard progressions. The first two are harmonic phrases with extended tertian chords. Progression c illustrates a $\frac{5-6}{3}$ sequence, and progression d is based on Chopin's Prelude no. 4. You should also practice the following progressions directly from the following examples in the textbook: examples 27.13a and b (two *fonte* sequences), examples 27.14a and b (two *monte* sequences), and examples 27.16b and c (two descending 5–6 sequences).

♩ Example 27.9

Chapter 28

The German Romantic *Lied*: Chromatic Harmony in Context

EXERCISE 28.1   Write a short analytical paper on Schubert's song "Auf dem Flusse," from *Die Winterreise,* no. 7 (anthology, no. 42). Turn in an annotated copy of the score.

1. First, study the poem. Does the text establish two different levels of reality? What are they? How are they parallel?

2. Mark the stanzas on the music.

3. Then, analyze the tonal content of the song, with special emphasis on the following passages:

   a) Analyze mm. 7–14, indicating the pivot chord or other modulating procedures (such as common tones) between the two keys in mm. 8–9 and 12–14.

   b) The same modulation appears again in mm. 43–47. But now, in m. 47, the D♯m chord is altered to function as a chromatic pivot to a new key. Analyze this modulation carefully. How is the new key related (by RN [Roman numeral]) to the original key of Em?

   c) Explain the series of modulations in mm. 54–62.

4. Discuss the relationship between text and music in this song.

   a) How does the text in the first stanza set a duality of mood? How is it reflected in the music?

   b) What is the mood of the third and fourth stanzas, and how is it portrayed musically?

   c) The fifth stanza, on the other hand, describes a state of turbulence. This state is expressed musically in a variety of ways. Explain. What key relationship does Schubert favor in this section of emotional turbulence?

EXERCISE 28.2   On your own music paper, write two successive modulations using the same chords and procedures as Schubert does in mm. 41–50 of "Auf dem Flusse." That is, modulate from Em to D♯m and on to G♯m. Write this exercise in four voices, and include a RN analysis with indication of pivot chords. Attach this exercise to your paper on the Schubert song.

EXERCISE 28.3   Write V⁺, and resolve it to i, in Gm. This chord may be used to modulate to two other minor keys by respelling it enharmonically. Indicate the keys, and provide the spelling (leaving the chord in the same position) and the correct resolution to the tonic in each of the new keys.

Key 1: Gm   **Key 2:**   **Key 3:**

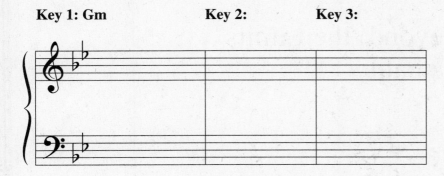

EXERCISE 28.4   Write a modulation in four voices by enharmonic reinterpretation of V⁺, from BM to a key of your choice.

BM:

KEYBOARD PROGRESSIONS   Practice the keyboard progression from example 28.1 in a variety of keys. Hear and understand the modulations by enharmonic reinterpretation of V⁺.

♪♪ Example 28.1

Chapter 29

Toward (and Beyond) the Limits of Functional Tonality

EXERCISE 29.1 Analysis.

1. Example 29.1.

    a) On a separate sheet, write a brief essay explaining tonal ambiguity in this example. How is F♯m implied? Is it ever established? Does the term "double-tonic complex" apply to this song? A translation of Heine's poem on which the song is based is provided. How do the tonal characteristics of this song reflect the meaning of the poem?

Example 29.1   R. Schumann, "Im wundershönen Monat Mai," from *Dichterliebe,* op. 48, mm. 14–26.

"In the beautiful month of May"

In the beautiful month of May
When all the buds were bursting.
Then within my heart
Love unfolded too.

In the beautiful month of May,
When all the birds were singing,
then I confessed to her
My longing and desire.

2. Example 29.2. On a separate sheet, write a brief essay on this example, discussing the following matters:

   a) Explain the tonality of this excerpt. In what key area can mm. 1–4 best be analyzed? And mm. 5–7? How are these keys established (if they are)? Can the sonorities be analyzed functionally, linearly, or both? What are the elements of tonal ambiguity?

   b) How does melody obscure harmony in this example?

   c) Provide a harmonic reduction for the complete passage, clearly showing chordal sonorities, voice leading, and nonchord tones. Provide a RN (Roman numeral) analysis of your reduction.

   d) This symphony dates from 1896. What specific influences from Wagner and *Tristan* can you identify in this fragment?

Example 29.2   A. Bruckner, Symphony no. 9, III, mm. 1–7

3. Comment on key area relationships in the following example.

♪♪ Example 29.3   Hugo Wolf, "Die ihr schwebet," from *Spanisches Liederbuch,* mm. 1–12

♪ Example 29.3   Continued

EXERCISE 29.2 Write two phrases for piano (melody and harmonic accompaniment), in A♭M and C♯m, respectively. Base your phrases on progressions that divide the octave symmetrically.

KEYBOARD PROGRESSIONS Practice the following keyboard progressions. Progression a is modeled after Wagner's *Tristan* prelude harmony, and progressions b, c, and d are based on equal divisions of the octave.

♪♪ Example 29.4

Chapter 30

Nonfunctional Pitch Centricity

EXERCISE 30.1   Analysis.

1. a) Using a diagram similar to the one found in example 30.4 in the book, explain how the triads in the following example are related by PLR trans-formations.

Example 30.1   F. Chopin, Ballade no. 1 in Gm, op. 23, mm. 90–95

b) The following example represents the succession of triads (key areas) in the cantabile section of Verdi's aria "Ah! sì, ben mio." Using a diagram, explain how the consonant triads in this example are related by PLR transformations.

♪ Example 30.2   G. Verdi, "Ah! sì, ben mio," from *Il trovatore,* Act III, mm. 1–22

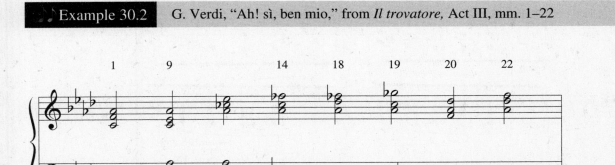

2. a) What harmonic or voice-leading technique is used in example 30.3a? And in example 30.3b? What is the difference between the way this technique is used in each of these examples?

b) What kind of chords are featured in example 30.3c?

♪ Example 30.3a   Claude Debussy, "Sarabande," from *Pour le piano,* mm. 1–4

Example 30.3b   mm. 11–12

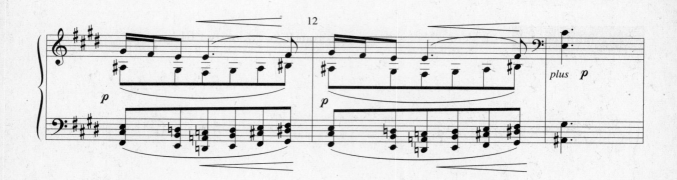

Example 30.3c   mm. 23–29

3. Determine the scale or pitch collection on which each of the following passages is based. In the examples of octatonic collections, determine whether the scale belongs to the S–T–S–T or the T–S–T–S type.

   a) Example 30.4.

♪♪ Example 30.4   C. Debussy, "Voiles," from *Preludes,* Book I, mm. 42–47

b) Example 30.5.

    1) Measures 45–47 (left hand only):

    2) Measures 48–51 (all pitches):

♪♪ Example 30.5   C. Debussy, "Reflects dans l'eau," from *Images,* mm. 45–51

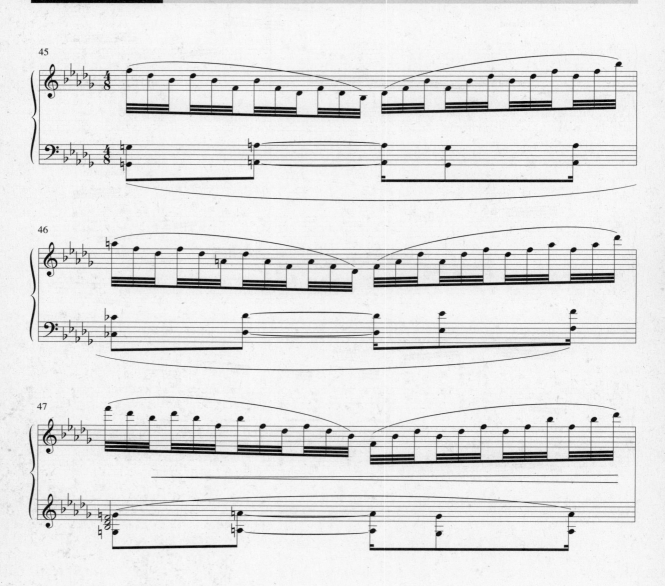

c) Example 30.6.

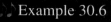 Example 30.6   B. Bartók, "Song of the Harvest," from *Forty-four Violin Duets,* no. 33, mm. 21–29

d) Example 30.7.

Example 30.7   B. Bartók, "From the Island of Bali," from *Mikrokosmos,* no. 109, mm. 1–11

EXERCISE 30.2   Write a phrase for piano (melody and accompaniment) based on a PL parsimonious progression, beginning on an E♭M triad. (For this and the following exercises, use your own music paper.)

EXERCISE 30.3   Write a phrase for piano (melody and accompaniment) based on an LR parsimonious progression, beginning on a DM triad.

EXERCISE 30.4   Write three melodies using the following scales: (1) Dorian, (2) Mixolydian, and (3) pentatonic. Craft the motivic and periodic structures of your melodies carefully (refer to the melodies in example 30.14 of the textbook as models).

EXERCISE 30.5   Write two phrases (melody and harmonic accompaniment) using the following harmonic techniques: (1) chromatic planing, and (2) quintal chords.

EXERCISE 30.6   Write a fragment for piano using an octatonic scale. You can write a melody with harmonic accompaniment (with chords derived from the octatonic scale), or a two-voice contrapuntal texture in an imitative style modeled after example 30.11 in the textbook.

KEYBOARD PROGRESSIONS

1. Practice the following PL, PR, and RL progressions directly from examples in the textbook: examples 30.4a, 30.5b, and 30.7a, respectively.

2. Practice the following progressions from example 30.8 in the textbook (Debussy's "The Sunken Cathedral"): mm. 14–15 (quintal chords), mm. 84–86 (quartal chords), mm 28–32 (diatonic planing), and mm. 62–65 (chromatic planing). Then, practice the following progressions based on Debussy examples discussed in this chapter.

Example 30.8

Harmony in Context Anthology

Harmony in

Anthology 1   **Tomás Luis de Victoria** (1548–1611), "Kyrie," from *Missa O magnum mysterium*

Anthology 1   Continued

Anthology 2   **Johann Jakob Walther** (1650–1717), Chorale Prelude, "Ach Gott und Herr," Verse 6

♪♪Anthology 3   Henry Purcell (1659–1695), "Ah, Belinda," from *Dido and Aeneas*

Anthology 3   Continued

Peace and I are stran - gers grown, Peace and I are stran - gers. stran - gers grown.

Anthology 4   **Friedrich Wilhelm Zachau** (1663–1712), Chorale Prelude, "In dich hab ich gehoffet, Herr"

Anthology 5   **Antonio Vivaldi** (1678–1741), Concerto in GM for Violin, Strings, and Continuo from *L'estro armonico*, op. 3, no. 3, II (Keyboard Reduction)

♪♪ Anthology 6   *Notebook for Anna Magdalena Bach* (1725), Minuet

♪♪ Anthology 7   *Notebook for Anna Magdalena Bach* (1725), Polonaise

♪♪ Anthology 8   **Johann Sebastian Bach** (1685–1750), Chorale 41, "Was mein Gott will, das g'scheh allzeit"

Anthology 9   **Johann Sebastian Bach** (1685–1750), Chorale 65, "Was Gott tut, das ist wohlgetan"

Anthology 10   **Johann Sebastian Bach** (1685–1750), Chorales 29, 64, and 76, "Freu' dich sehr, o meine Seele"

Anthology 11   **Johann Sebastian Bach** (1685–1750), Minuet, from French Suite no. 3 in Bm

Menuet

Anthology 12   Johann Sebastian Bach (1685–1750), Gavotte, from French Suite no. 5 in GM

George Frideric Handel (1685–1759), "Lascia ch'io pianga," from *Rinaldo*

(Fine)

Almirena
Il duo - lo in - fran - ga   que - ste ri - tor - te,   de' miei mar - ti - ri sol

per pie - ta,   de' miei mar - ti - ri sol per pie - tà.

Aria da capo

Let me bewail   Let [my] suffering break
my cruel fate,   the bonds
and [let me] sigh   of my torments
for liberty!   through [the power] of pity.

Anthology 17   **George Frideric Handel** (1685–1759), "Amaz'd to Find the Foe So Near," from *Belshazzar*

♪♪ Anthology 17   Continued

maz'd   to find   the foe— so— near,   a   maz'd to find the foe_____

_____ so   near,   when sleep_____ and wine   their

sen - ses drown,   all hearts   shall faint   and melt   with fear,   all hands   un - nerv'd   fall

Adagio   **[Tempo I]**

feeb - ly down,   all hands un-nerv'd   fall   feeb - ly down.

Adagio   **[Tempo I]**

Anthology 18   **Anna Amalie** (1723–1787), Sonata for Flute in FM, I, mm. 1–21

Anthology 19   **Joseph Haydn** (1732–1809), Minuet and Trio, from Divertimento in CM, Hob. XVI:1

Menuet da capo

Anthology 20   **Joseph Haydn** (1732–1809), Piano Sonata in DM, Hob. XVI:24, II, mm. 1–24

♪♪ Anthology 20   Continued

♪♪ Anthology 21   Joseph Haydn (1732–1809), Piano Sonata in DM, Hob. XVI:37, III

Finale.
Presto, ma non troppo.

♪♪ Anthology 21   Continued

Joseph Boulogne, Chevalier de Saint–Georges (1739–1799), Violin
Concerto no. 1 in GM, I, mm. 1–12

Anthology 23   **Joseph Boulogne, Chevalier de Saint–Georges** (1739–1799), Symphonie
Concertante in AM, op. 10, no. 2, II, mm. 1–24

Anthology 25   Continued

♪♪ Anthology 25   Continued

♪♪ Anthology 27   **Wolfgang Amadeus Mozart** (1756–1791), Piano Sonata in AM, K. 331, I

Anthology 27   Continued

Anthology 27   Continued

🎵♪♪ Anthology 27   Continued

Anthology 27   Continued

VAR. VI

Allegro

♪♪♪ Anthology 27 · Continued

Anthology 28   **Wolfgang Amadeus Mozart** (1756–1791), Piano Sonata in B♭M, K. 333, III

♪♪♪ Anthology 28   Continued

♪♪ Anthology 28   Continued

♪♪ Anthology 28   Continued

♪♪ Anthology 28   Continued

♪♪ Anthology 28   Continued

♪♪ Anthology 28   Continued

♪♪ Anthology 28   Continued

♪♪ Anthology 28   Continued

♪ Anthology 29   **Wolfgang Amadeus Mozart** (1756–1791), "Wie Unglücklich bin ich nit,"
K. 147

Wie un - glück - lich bin ich nit, wie schmach - tend sind mei - ne Tritt', wenn

ich mich nach dir len - ke. Nur die Seuf - zer trö - sten mich, al - le Schmer - zen

häu - fen sich, wenn ich auf dich ge - den - ke, wenn ich auf

dich ge - den - ke.

How unhappy I am,
How languishing are my steps,
When I turn them towards you.

Only my sighs console me,
All my pains multiply
When I think of you.

Why should I ask for money and goods
If I am happy!
If God just gives me health,
I'll have a happy mind
and sing my morning and evensong in a thankful spirit

♪♪ Anthology 31   Maria Theresia von Paradis (1759–1824), *Sicilienne*

♪♪ Anthology 32   **Ludwig van Beethoven** (1770–1827), Piano Sonata in Fm, op. 2, no. 1, I and III

Anthology 32   Continued

Anthology 32   Continued

♪ Anthology 32   Continued

♪♪ Anthology 33   **Ludwig van Beethoven** (1770–1827), Piano Sonata in Cm, op. 10, no. 1, II, mm. 1–16

♪♪ Anthology 34   Ludwig van Beethoven (1770–1827), Piano Sonata in Cm, op. 13, III

Anthology 34   Continued

♪ Anthology 34   Continued

Anthology 34   Continued

Anthology 34   Continued

Anthology 34   Continued

Anthology 34   Continued

♪♪ Anthology 34   Continued

♪♪ Anthology 35   **Ludwig van Beethoven** (1770–1827), Piano Sonata in CM, op. 53, *Waldstein*, I

♪♪ Anthology 35   Continued

Anthology 35   Continued

# 332   ANTHOLOGY

♪♪ Anthology 35   Continued

Anthology 35   Continued

Anthology 35 Continued

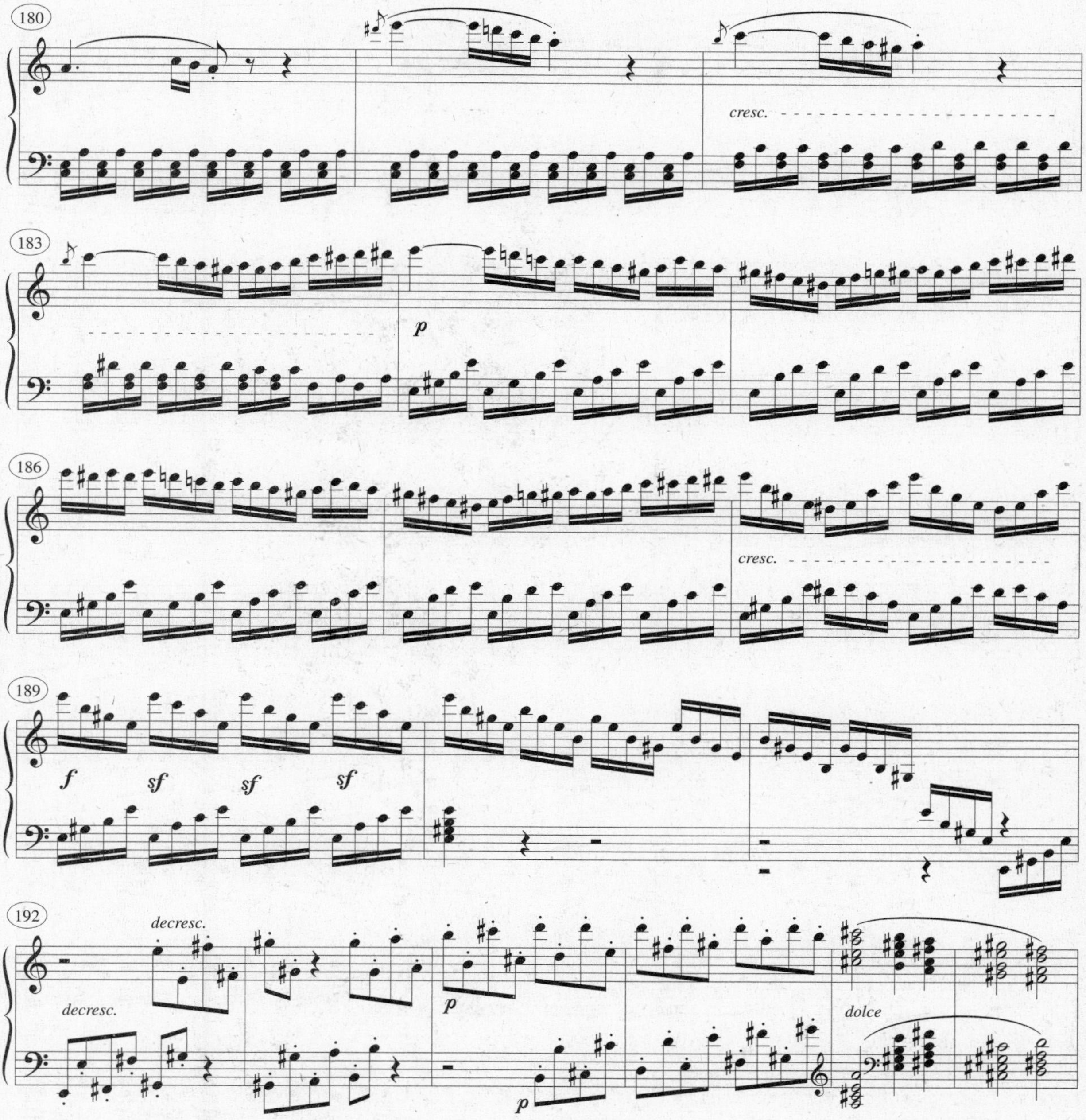

♪♪ Anthology 35   Continued

♪♪ Anthology 35   Continued

♩♪ Anthology 35   Continued

♪♪ Anthology 35   Continued

♪♪ Anthology 35   Continued

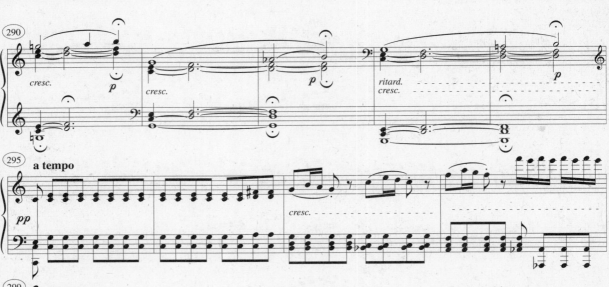

♪♪ Anthology 36   **Ludwig van Beethoven** (1770–1827), Piano Sonata in E♭M, op. 7, II, mm.15–58

♪♪ Anthology 36   Continued

Anthology 37   **Friedrich Kuhlau** (1786–1832), Piano Sonatina in FM, op. 55/4, II

♪♪ Anthology 38   Franz Schubert (1797–1828), *Erlkönig*, op. 1

♪♪ Anthology 38   Continued

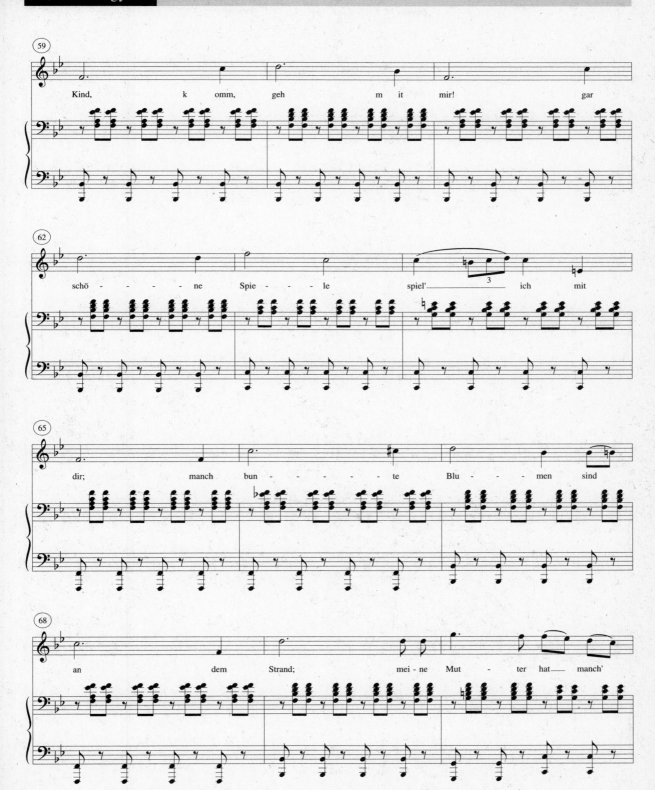

Anthology 38   Continued

Sohn, ich seh es ge - nau; es schein - en die al - ten Wei - den so

grau.   "Ich

lie - be dich, mich reizt dei - ne schö - ne Ge - stalt; und bist du nicht wil - lig, so

brauch ich Ge - walt".   Main Va - ter, main Va - ter, jetzt fasst er mich

Anthology 38   Continued

127 an! Erl - kö - nig hat mir ein Leids ge - than!

132 *accelerando* Dem Va - ter grau - set's, er rei - tet gesch - *cresc.*

136 wind, er hält in Ar - men das äch - zen - de

140 Kind, er - reicht den Hof mit Müh und

Anthology 38   Continued

Who rides so late through night and wind?
It is a father with his child;
He holds the boy in his arm,
He clasps him tight, he keeps him warm.

"My son, why hidest thy face in fear?"
"Seest thou not, Father, the Erlking?
The Erlking with crown and train?"
"My son, 'tis but a streak of mist."

"O dear child, come away with me!
Lovely games I'll play with thee!
Many-colored flowers grow by the shore,
My mother has many golden robes."

"My father, my father, hearest thou not
What Erlking softly promises me?"
"Be calm, be calm, my child;

"Fair boy, wilt thou come with me?
My lovely daughters shall wait on thee;
My daughters keep their nightly revels;
They will rock thee, dance, and sing thee to sleep."

"My father, my father, seest thou not
Erlking's daughters in that dark place?"
"My son, my son, I see clearly;
It is only the gleam of the old gray willows."

"I love thee, thy fair form ravishes me;
And if thou art not willing, I'll take thee by force."
"My father, my father, now he is seizing me!
Erlking has done me harm!"

The father shudders, he rides fast,
And holds in his arm the moaning child;
He reaches home with effort and toil:
In his arms the child lay dead!

Anthology 39   **Franz Schubert** (1797–1828), Waltz, op. 9, no. 14

Franz Schubert (1797–1828), Ecossaise no. 2, from *Waltzer, Ländler und Ecossaisen*, op. 18

Anthology 42   **Franz Schubert** (1797–1828), "Auf dem Flusse," from *Die Winterreise*

On the Stream

You that were once so merry,
You leaping laughing burn,
Are fallen into silence,
No greeting you return.

With crust all hard and frozen
You now are overspread.
You lie there cold and moveless
Upon your sandy bed.

I'll take a sharp-edged pebble,
And on your surface white
The name of my beloved
With hour and day I'll write.

The day of our first greeting,
The day when last we met.
And round the name and fingers
A broken ring I'll set.

My heart, within this
brooklet
Do you your image know?
Beneath its frozen surface
How turbulent its flow!
Ah, how turbulent its flow!

Anthology 43   **Fanny Mendelssohn Hensel** (1805–1847), "Bitte," from *Six Songs*, op. 7

Gaze on me for a while you dark eye, bring your full power into play, earnest, gentle, dreamy, unfathomable sweet night.
Take with your magic darkness this world away from me, that over my life you alone shall hover for ever and for ever.

Anthology 45   **Frédéric Chopin** (1810–1849), Mazurka 49 in Fm, op. posth. 68, no. 4

Anthology 46   **Robert Schumann** (1810–1856), Kinder Sonate no. 1, from *Three Piano Sonatas for the Young*, op. 118a

Anthology 46   Continued

♪♪ Anthology 47   **Robert Schumann** (1810–1856), "Ich grolle nicht," from *Dichterliebe*, op. 48, mm. 1–19

Nicht zu schnell

mf

Ich grol - le nicht   und wenn das Herz_____ auch

④

bricht,   e - wig ver-lor' - nes Lieb,   e - wig ver-lor' - nes

⑧

Lieb!_____   ich grol - - - le nicht,   ich grol - - - le

♪♪ Anthology 47   Continued

nicht.   Wie du auch strahlst   in Di - a - man - ten - pracht,   es fällt kein

Strahl   in dei - nes   Herz - ens Nacht,   das weiß ich   längst.

I hold no resentment,
And even if my heart breaks,
O love forever lost,
I hold no resentment.
And although you gleam in jewelled splendor,
There falls no ray upon your heart's night,
I've long known it.

Anthology 48   **Robert Schumann** (1810–1856), "Widmung," from *Myrthen*, op. 25

You, my soul, you my heart,
You, my delight, you, my grief,
You, my world, in which I live,
You my heaven, into which I soar,
O you my grave, in which forever
I have laid my sorrow!
You are the rest, you are the peace,
You are sent from heaven to me.
That you love me makes me worthy,
Your glance has transfigured me,
Your love lifts me above myself,
My good spirit, my better self!

You, my soul, you my heart,
You, my delight, you, my grief,
You, my world, in which I live,
You my heaven, into which I soar,
My good spirit, my better self!

Anthology 49   Robert Schumann (1810–1856), "Am leuchtenden Sommermorgen," from *Dichterliebe*, op. 48

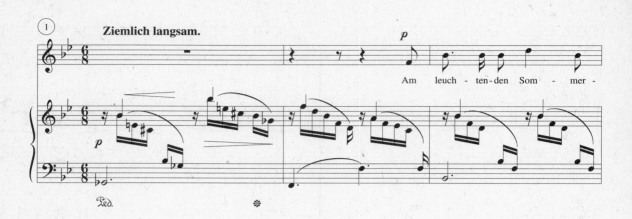

"On a bright summer morning"

On a bright summer morning
I walk around the garden.
The flowers are whispering and speaking,
But I walk in silence.

The flowers are whispering and speaking,
and they look with pity on me;
Be not angry with our sister,
You sorrowful, pale man.

Robert Schumann (1810–1856), "Folk Song," from *Album for the Young*, op. 68, mm. 1–8

Im klagenden Ton

Anthology 51   Franz Liszt (1811–1886), *Consolation* no. 4

Anthology 52   **Giuseppe Verdi** (1813–1901), "Libiamo ne'lieti calici," from *La traviata*, mm. 22–42

Let's drink of the joyful goblets
That beauty adorns with flowers
And the fleeting hour will get drunk
With sensual pleasure

Anthology 53   **Giuseppe Verdi** (1813–1901), *Il trovatore*, Act II, no. 11, mm. 1–11

Azucena: plunge this blade up to the hilt into the heart of the cruel one.
Strike!
Manrico: Yes, I swear it. This blade will descend into the heart of the cruel one.

♪♪ Anthology 54   Giuseppe Verdi (1813–1901), *Il trovatore*, Act II, no. 14, mm. 15–24

Me! I turn to Him
Who alone can dry the mourner's tears
of sorrow, and when my days of
grief are over, mercy eternal may
guide my weary spirit
yet to meet him again.

cin - to___   dir - ti: per te ho pu - gna - to,   per te ho vin - to!
splen - dor,   say - ing: For you I con - quered.   See your de - fend - er!

Andantino. (♩ = 116)
con espress.

Ce - le - ste A - i - da,___
Fair - est A - i - da,___

Anthology 57   **Hugo Wolf** (1860–1903), "Das verlassene Mägdlein," from *Gedichte von Mörike*, no. 7

21

etwas lebhafter

in Leid ver - sun - ken   Plötz - lich,   da

28

etwas ruhiger

kommt es mir,   treu - lo - ser Kna - be,   dass ich die Nacht von dir ge -

33

wie zu Anfang

träu - met ha - be.   Trä - ne auf

Trä - ne dann stür - zet her - nie - der; so kommt der Tag her - an o ging' er

wie - der!

ppp

Early, when the cocks crow,
Before the stars fade out,
I must stand at the hearth
And light the fire.

Lovely is the flames' light
With its flying sparks;
I gaze into it,
Deep in sorrow.

Suddenly I remember,
Faithless boy,
That I in the night
Of thee have dreamed.

Tear on tear
Tumbles down;
So begins the day—
O, would it were ended!

Richard Strauss (1864–1949), "Ruhe, meine Seele!," op. 27, no. 1

 Anthology 59   **Amy Beach** (1867–1944), *Ecstasy*

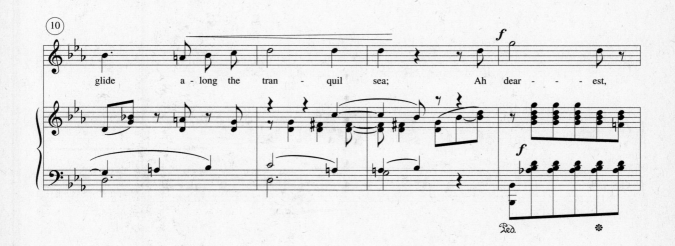

dear - est,   have   we   not   to - geth - er   One long,   bright

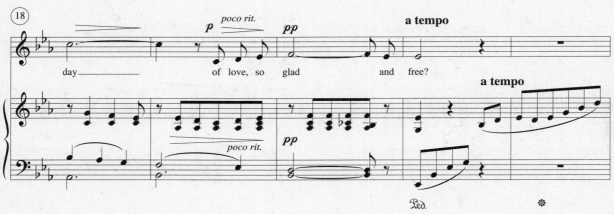

day_____   of love, so   glad   and   free?

On - ly   to

♪ Anthology 59 Continued

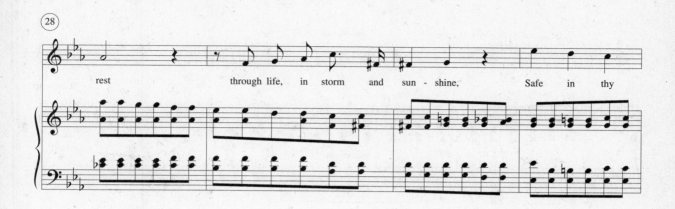

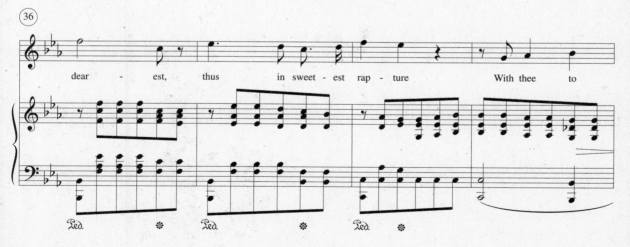

live,_____   with thee at last   to die!_____

Anthology 60

Igor Stravinsky (1882–1971), "Danses des adolescentes," from *The Rite of Spring*, mm. 1–13